Ca$h
On
D€liver¥

A new approach to foreign aid

Nancy Birdsall and William D. Savedoff
with Ayah Mahgoub and Katherine Vyborny

With an application
to primary schooling

Center for Global Development

Library of Congress Cataloging-in-Publication Data

Birdsall, Nancy.

  Cash on delivery : a new approach to foreign aid : an application to primary schooling / Nancy Birdsall and William D. Savedoff.

      p. cm.

  Includes bibliographical references.

  ISBN 978-1-933286-36-5

  eISBN 978-1-933286-49-5

  1. Economic assistance—Developing countries. 2. Education, Primary—Developing countries. 3. Developing countries—Economic policy. I. Savedoff, William D. II. Title.

  HC60.B524 2009

  338.9109172′4--dc22

                                2008052413

Cover photo by Harvey Nelson/Courtesy of Photoshare.

Editing and typesetting by Communications Development Incorporated, Washington, D.C.

Contents

Preface and acknowledgments   v

Part I
A proposal for Cash on Delivery Aid   1

Chapter 1
Buying things versus buying development   3

Chapter 2
A solution: Cash on Delivery Aid   17

Part II
Applications of Cash on Delivery Aid

Chapter 3
**Applying COD Aid to primary education: a
contract between partners**   45

Chapter 4
**Applying COD Aid to primary education:
funding and implementation**   67

Chapter 5
Learning what works: the research challenge   75

Chapter 6
Federal systems: a COD Aid proposal for Mexico's
upper secondary schools   87

Chapter 7
Beyond primary education: COD Aid for
other development goals   97

References   105

Appendix
Term sheets for COD Aid contracts   111

Index   119

Preface and acknowledgments

Since its inception, the Center for Global Development has put a premium on translating independent research into practical ideas. This book is firmly in that tradition. It is part of a broader initiative I have led at the Center—with enthusiasm and with increasing passion—to develop and disseminate a simple and practical approach to development aid that can help official and private funders realize the reforms they have promised on paper but failed to deliver on the ground. The approach is called, simply but revealingly, Cash on Delivery Aid.

Even the fiercest aid critics recognize that some aid programs bring results: millions of lives have been saved and millions of children educated because of aid programs. But tougher questions remain: has aid helped—can it help—strengthen the institutions of an effective and responsible state that eventually provides services by, for, and with its citizens on its own? Does aid in some settings actually makes things worse by, for example, short-circuiting state building (for instance, reducing the incentive for tax collection) and sustaining corrupt or ineffective governments? Even "good" aid to responsible states has come into question. As aid has become an increasingly complicated and difficult business—with unhealthy competition among funders and high transaction costs for aid-dependent governments—has the aid system itself become a constraint on state-building? As aid-dependent governments focus on satisfying the demands of their donors rather than those of their own citizens, has aid set back the elusive process of building state institutions that are responsive to their own citizens?

Friends of aid argue that aid is less politicized now than it was during the Cold War and that the official donors are making progress fixing the system's problems: fragmentation, lack of coordination, lack of ownership, lack of alignment with recipient-country priorities, lack of transparency, lack of results, lack of evidence about results, and more lacks! But insiders know that progress is painfully slow and, in many low-income countries, worryingly reversible.

The Cash on Delivery Aid (COD Aid) approach presented in this book is designed to allow funders and recipients to escape the "lacks" of the system listed above. Mostly it allows funders to escape the trap that many aid programs create, a trap that makes recipients responsible to funders for inputs instead of to its own citizens for development outcomes.

COD Aid builds on a rich body of earlier work on aid effectiveness at the Center: on debt relief and reduction with its implications for the larger aid architecture (*Delivering on Debt Relief*), on demonstrably effective large-scale international public health programs (*Millions Saved*), on use of aid for performance incentives to nongovernmental organizations and households (*Performance Incentives in Public Health*), on the seven sins of donors and what to do about them (*Reinventing Foreign Aid*), on why evaluation doesn't get done (*Evaluation Gap*), on the Millennium Development goals (*The Trouble with the MDGs*), on aid and growth (*Counting Chickens When They Hatch*), on rethinking the U.S. foreign assistance program, on advance market commitments (contingent spending in the rich world buying measurable gains in the poor world), on aid and institutions (*After the Big Push?*), and more.

Like so many good ideas, this one began with a short note I received from Owen Barder, at the time a part-time staff member at the Center. That note led to a jointly authored 2006 CGD working paper, "Payments for Progress: A Hands-Off Approach to Foreign Aid." In 2007, I joined forces with CGD visiting fellow William Savedoff to further refine the idea. We began a comprehensive process of research and consultation to further develop and improve it. We undertook new research, commissioned background papers from experts, interviewed dozens of practitioners, and engaged in extensive consultations with officials, technical experts, and civil-society representatives. We convened meetings to discuss our proposal and participated in events sponsored by others to present our work and receive feedback and insights on what to take into account when refining the idea. From a good idea to the challenges of a practical program has been a long and still unfinished journey of discovery and learning in itself.

In this book we present the results of our work so far. We do so in the spirit of matchmaker, hoping our work will bring together funders and aid-receiving governments. In Part I, we situate the literature on whether aid is effective within the realm of questions about the shortcomings of the system. We then describe our idea, COD Aid, as a new kind of delivery mechanism for aid that we believe addresses the inherent problems with transfers of any kind from a funder (bilateral or multilateral official agency or private foundation) to a recipient (a government or major program implementer). In Part II, we apply the approach to primary education, showing one example of how the approach could be practically implemented. We also briefly propose applications of COD Aid to other sectors. Ultimately, the parents of this approach (country and donor partners) will decide how to raise it, but we hope this book will serve as a practical guide.

This book and our initiative are a result of the generous and immensely valuable input of many people over the past few years. My coauthors and I would like to extend a very special thanks to several individuals. First we thank Owen Barder whose keen thinking and commitment to making aid work started us down this path. We are immensely grateful for the valuable insights and stellar advocacy of Desmond Bermingham, Ambassador Mark Green, Robin Horn, CGD Board member Ngozi Okonjo-Iweala, Elizabeth King, Nancy Lee, Rakesh Rajani, Smita Singh, and Alcyone Vasconcelos. Their guidance and outreach were and continue to be critical to the enhancement of our proposal and to sharing the idea with a broad audience. We would also like to extend a special thanks to President Jakaya Kikwete of Tanzania, Kofi Annan, and Minister Maghembe of Liberia for their strong support and their request for donors to try COD Aid.

The ideas in this book were shaped by the excellent background papers prepared for this initiative by Maurice Boissiere, Luis Crouch, Paolo de Renzio, Merilee Grindle, Marlaine Lockheed, Jonathan Mitchell, Michael Woolcock, and Ngaire Woods. We also extend sincere thanks to our colleagues Satish Chand, Mead Over, and April Harding for both their contributions to this proposal and to alternative applications of COD Aid.

We are grateful for valuable feedback on initial drafts of this book from many people, including Jenny Aker, Marcelo Cabrol, Michael Clemens, Homi Kharas, Vijaya Ramachandran, David Roodman, Ana Santiago, and Nicolas van de Walle. We appreciate the openness of the Mexican government in allowing us to publish the results of a workshop at which we assessed the possibility of applying COD Aid to intranational transfers.

We are grateful for the feedback and guidance of countless other people, but especially to that of K.Y. Amoako, Jean Arkedis, Tayani Banda, Amie Batson, Luis Benveniste, Nicolas Burnett, Robin Davies, Mourad Ezzine, Linda Frey, James Habyarimana, Brian Hanssen, Nigel Harris, Harry Hatry, Ward Heneveld, Sheila Herrling, George Ingram, Pierre Jacquet, Lars Johannes, Michael Keating, Elizabeth King, Timo Mahn, Jeremy Mark, William Masters, Nadim Matta, Gavin McGillivray, Lynn Murphy, Carmen Nonay, Marianna Ofosu, Patrick Osakwe, Richard Parr, Claudia Pieterse, Mary Joy Pigozzi, Alice Poole, Ben Power, Lant Pritchett, Olivier Ray, Sonal Shah, Sarah Jane Staats, Miguel Szekely, Binh Thanh Vu, Patricia Veevers-Carter, and Jane Wales.

We also appreciate how much the analysis and design were improved by listening to the comments, critiques and ideas that were offered by so many people who gave their time, expertise, and encouragement at meetings at the UN Economic Commission for

Africa in Addis Ababa, Ethiopia; at the Meeting of European Union Member States Education Experts in Brussels, Belgium; at the Education for All–Fast Track Initiative Technical Meeting in Dakar, Senegal; with the Development Partner group in Dar es Salaam, Tanzania; at the UN Follow-up International Conference on Financing for Development to Review the Monterrey Consensus in Doha, Qatar; at the World Bank and International Monetary Fund Annual Meeting in Istanbul, Turkey; at the U.K. Department for International Development in London, United Kingdom; at the Ministry of Education and Mexicanos Primeros in Mexico City, Mexico; at the Hemispheric Think Thank Meeting and at the Canadian International Development Agency in Ottawa, Canada; at the AidWatch launch in New York City, United States; at the Sixth Plenary Meeting of the Leading Group on Financing for Development in Paris, France; at the Eighth Annual Global Philanthropy Forum, Washington, D.C., United States; at meetings and seminars at the Johns Hopkins School for Advanced International Studies, the Brookings Institution, the World Bank, the Inter-American Development Bank, the U.S. State Department, and other organizations in Washington, D.C., United States; and at many other meetings in Lilongwe, Malawi; Addis Ababa, Ethiopia; and Stockholm, Sweden. We appreciate as well the numerous private interviews and email exchanges that informed this book.

We are grateful to Lawrence MacDonald for his continued feedback and guidance on many aspects of the initiative, and for his creativity in naming our idea Cash on Delivery Aid. John Osterman was generous with his guidance and helped shepherd the book to completion—we are very grateful for his help. We want to express our appreciation to Amy Smith for unraveling some of the more complicated arguments and her professional and comprehensive editing.

The work of this book and this initiative are coming to fruition through the generous support of the William and Flora Hewlett Foundation.

Any remaining errors are our full responsibility—and an opportunity for you to further advance these ideas!

Nancy Birdsall
President
Center for Global Development
January 2010

A proposal for
Cash on Delivery Aid

Part I

Buying things versus buying development

Foreign aid has become a big and difficult business. In the last decade, official aid has grown faster than ever.[1] In 2000, the international community committed itself to help developing countries achieve the Millennium Development Goals. As part of this commitment, developed countries promised to increase foreign aid substantially—doubling or, for Africa, tripling their annual aid flows.[2] Foreign aid has grown significantly since 2000, especially if debt relief for the poorest countries is included. By 2007, it amounted to more than $120 billion a year (figure 1.1). In the same period, private giving in support of nonprofit and philanthropic international programs also rose substantially.

Despite this impressive infusion of resources, the flow of aid now faces two big challenges. One is whether economic recession in funder countries will undercut official commitments to provide more aid. The second is whether the sheer number of public and private funders with multiple objectives, procedures, and cultures will fragment and further weaken what has always been fragile public support for aid. Aid going directly to governments in low-income countries seems at greatest risk of losing public confidence.

We believe that aid, both public and private, can make a difference in improving lives in poor countries. We also believe that the willingness of taxpayers and private funders to finance aid programs depends more than ever on evidence that aid programs deliver. To keep public support, aid programs must help generate measurable progress on some dimensions in aid-recipient countries. In response to the growing pressure to show that aid can deliver, official and private funders have already begun to implement various approaches to aid that pays for results. This book, building on concepts first proposed in Barder and Birdsall (2006) and benefiting from the experience

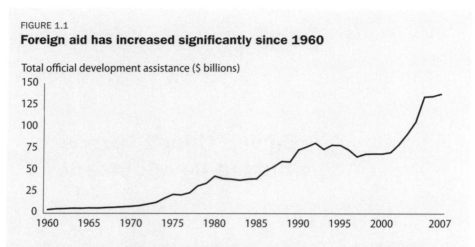

FIGURE 1.1
Foreign aid has increased significantly since 1960

Total official development assistance ($ billions)

Note: The figure depicts the growth of foreign aid for all donors using data on total net of-ficial development assistance flows.
Source: OECD Stat Extracts, Table 2a.

of current efforts, explores a results-based approach and takes it an ambitious step further.

In this chapter we assess the fundamental shortcomings of the current aid system and the fairly limited success of reform programs to address them. In the next, we outline our proposal for what we call Cash on Delivery Aid (COD Aid).

Aid and its critics

For all the good that foreign aid can do in vaccinating children or building schools and roads, aid has never been without its critics, who fall into two camps. Some argue that aid actually undermines development. Others—with whom we agree—believe that the foreign aid system can work, but only if seriously reformed.[3]

Critics in the first camp assert that foreign aid can undermine development in several ways. Aid inflows that are large relative to the local economy can inflate exchange rates and penalize a country's exports. Aid programs also increase demand for local people skilled in management and administration, thus competing with both the private sector and the government. This can result in a lack of management skills for administering not only aid programs but also all public functions (box 1.1). Aid can also reduce incentives to improve revenue collection, allow governments to delay difficult reforms, and encourage rent-seeking by powerful political and economic elites. And it can weaken or distort local political and other institutions by making a government accountable primarily to its foreign funders rather than to its citizens. Finally, some argue that aid can undermine a country's

> Critics in the first camp assert that foreign aid can undermine development in several ways

BOX 1.1
Administrative costs can burden recipients: Vietnam

Although foreign aid provides governments with additional funding to implement beneficial projects, the administrative costs of traditional aid can be substantial and burdensome for the public sector in recipient countries. In 2002, Vietnam received about $1.3 billion from about 44 official donors. An additional 350 international nongovernmental organizations (NGOs) contributed funds and operated in Vietnam that year.

Overall, foreign funding supported more than 8,000 development projects. Although these projects addressed critical needs of the Vietnamese people, they also imposed a large burden on Vietnamese officials, who were required to submit thousands of quarterly reports and host hundreds of donor visits that year. The demands on these officials to report to donors may have diverted their talent from other important functions.

Source: DAC2a ODA Disbursements Table, OECD Stat Extracts; Acharya, de Lima, and Moore 2003; Knack and Rahman 2004.

development by interrupting self-discovery, the process for countries to develop their own institutions and capacities for effective governance, strong economies and robust political systems through experiment and learning by doing.

Critics in the second camp recognize many of the same shortcomings. Rather than seeing these shortcomings as inherent to foreign aid, they see them as failings of the official global aid system—which, if seriously reformed, could work much better. For this second group of critics, foreign aid is too often designed to primarily serve domestic constituencies in funder countries. This leads to such detrimental practices as tied aid, requiring that aid be spent on the funder country's own products and services. They also note that the foreign aid system has high transaction costs. These result from the fragmentation of programs, a multitude of funders operating in any given country, a bias toward funder involvement in project design and implementation as the solution to weak local execution, and—as emphasized below—a focus on program inputs rather than on desired outcomes (less easily monitored and managed). Critics in the reformist camp also draw attention to domestic political and economic cycles in funder countries, amplifying volatility in foreign aid and hindering proper planning and implementation in recipient countries. Finally, these critics are concerned that funders have difficulty learning from their experiences—not only because evaluation is complicated and costly but also because aid proponents hesitate, with some justification, to advertise the limits of their craft.[4]

We believe that the concerns of both sets of critics overlap in many ways. For example, the accountability problem emphasized by those who think foreign aid is inherently flawed is closely associated with the focus on inputs, high transaction costs, and lack of local learning emphasized

Critics in the second camp see that the official global aid system, if seriously reformed, could work much better

by those who think aid can be reformed. We argue in the next chapter that most of these problems could be avoided if funders linked some of their aid to agreed-upon and measurable outcomes rather than inputs.

Past and current efforts to reform aid

Criticism of foreign aid has a long history. Funders have generated a variety of strategies in response, with mixed success. For many years, critics had argued that traditional investment loans were failing to help low- and middle-income countries develop because poor public policies constrained growth. In the 1980s, the World Bank and other official creditors responded to these concerns by introducing conditionality. Loans and grants were made on condition that a country adopt such public policies as fiscal discipline, monetary restraint, and more liberal trade and financial policies. Evidence mounted, however, that such conditions rarely succeeded. First, reforms were implemented only when governments were already committed to the policy reforms. Second, funders were often unwilling to enforce conditions, approving waivers or softening requirements rather than walking away from programs and governments they were anxious to continue supporting.[5] Doubts also grew about the value of the reforms themselves.[6] Although conditionality remains a part of the aid system, it has fallen out of favor as a response to the aid system's core problems.

In the mid-1990s, the World Bank and several bilateral aid agencies adopted process conditions as a next promising approach. On the premise that successful development demands domestic ownership and involvement in the design and implementation of programs, funders required recipient governments to engage in consultations, planning exercises, and assessments with the participation of nongovernmental organizations, local communities, and domestic interest groups. The most prominent example of these process conditions is the Poverty Reduction Strategy Paper, requiring that low-income countries seeking aid reach a broad consensus on public policies in many sectors with the involvement of local groups. This approach has not increased country ownership or aid effectiveness, even according to the World Bank's own evaluations.[7]

A recent response to the criticism has been to steer foreign aid away from specific projects and toward broader sectoral or national budget financing

A more recent response to the criticism has been to steer foreign aid away from specific projects and toward broader sectoral or national budget financing. This approach rewards responsible management with direct budget support. For example, the World Bank allocates its most concessional funding in part on indicators of good governance in low-income countries. Its policy-based loans support budget expenditures of recipient governments. The European Union and the U.K. government also provide budget support, paying unrestricted funds to the national treasuries of governments judged to have reasonably good expenditure management and adequate financial controls.

FIGURE 1.2
Traditional aid continues to dominate World Bank loans for primary education . . .

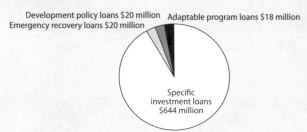

Development policy loans $20 million   Adaptable program loans $18 million
Emergency recovery loans $20 million

Specific
investment loans
$644 million

Note: Data are for fiscal 2008.
Source: World Bank, Human Development Network.

FIGURE 1.3
. . . and in countries that receive budget support, such as Malawi

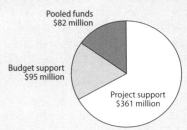

Pooled funds
$82 million

Budget support
$95 million

Project support
$361 million

Note: Data are for fiscal 2008.
Source: Malawi Ministry of Finance.

These reform strategies, especially budget support, have reduced the administrative burden on recipient governments and are more likely to encourage their ownership of programs. In that sense, they are a step in the right direction. But the strategies still cover a relatively small portion of total transfers, even for the World Bank (figures 1.2 and 1.3). Budget support and policy-based loans also continue to require substantial ongoing funder scrutiny of country spending and other management systems to minimize the risk of waste and corruption. In addition, they tend to be based on funders' judgments that the plans are adequate or policies acceptable, and thus do not fully empower recipients, and they make it hard for funders to reduce or withdraw support. Since clear measures of government performance are difficult to define ex ante, failure to meet them is difficult to establish ex post. Such failures cannot then be invoked as a reason to halt disbursements.[8] Moreover, budget support and policy-based loans are available only to a small group of eligible countries with demonstrated track records of good management. So, the approaches cannot be forward looking—or provide aid in countries where, despite honest and responsible leadership, the current limitations of administrative and financial management make them ineligible.[9]

As outside criticism of aid has continued and concerns have grown in official aid quarters, the major funders have articulated and begun to reform the overall aid system. The Paris Declaration, signed in 2005 by more than 90 countries and multilateral organizations, committed the major funders of foreign aid to an ambitious set of reforms, including:

- Increasing a recipient country's ownership of initiatives financed with foreign aid.
- Harmonizing the design, implementation, and reporting of foreign assistance by different organizations.
- Aligning foreign aid with the recipient country's priorities, systems, and procedures.
- Focusing on results and outcomes as measures of performance.
- Improving accountability of both funders and recipient countries for the effective use of foreign aid.
- Increasing the predictability of foreign aid to help recipient governments better plan and manage their own budgets.

So far, however, progress has been limited, as documented by official monitoring reports.[10]

Why has reform been so difficult, despite substantial resolve and attention on the part of aid officials in virtually all the major funder countries and in the World Bank and other multilateral organizations? What fundamental problems have the efforts so far failed to tackle effectively?

Why is foreign aid difficult to do well?

An enduring challenge of foreign aid is accountability. In countries that rely fully on tax revenue to finance government programs, taxpayers play a critical role in monitoring government behavior. They can observe the results or outcomes in, for example, road maintenance and school quality, and hold governments accountable for those results. But in countries that rely in part on aid, citizens lack similar incentives and mechanisms for monitoring and enforcing good government performance, particularly where democratic norms are not well established. Faced with this weak local accountability, funders tend to finance and monitor inputs, which are easier to track and come sooner in any program but are a poor proxy for the results or outcomes funders actually want to support. The fundamental problem of accountability in aid transfers is manifested in three forms.[11]

Aid programs and policies are only weakly accountable to citizens of funder countries

First, aid programs and policies are only weakly accountable to citizens of funder countries. These programs have multiple, often contradictory

goals and report little on their achievements, if at all. Although parlia-
ments may investigate and criticize programs, voters rarely base their elec-
toral decisions on aid effectiveness, which is only one small part of the
broader political debates in any country. This weak accountability opens
space for funding agencies and interest groups to modify foreign aid for
any number of legitimate or illegitimate goals—from geopolitical support and national security cooperation to policies favored on ideological
grounds and benefits for domestic corporations.

> **Aid programs and policies are even more weakly accountable to citizens of recipient countries**

Second, aid programs and policies are even more weakly account-
able to citizens of recipient countries. Rightly or wrongly, funders see themselves as
responsible for ensuring that foreign aid is used appropriately. They therefore insist on
determining the standards for setting priorities and for designing and monitoring programs. These standards reflect their own perspectives and requirements, even where
the recipient country's citizens can hold their governments accountable at the polls.
Since the citizens do not provide the funds for development programs, their interest
and ability to hold domestic politicians accountable for those funds is greatly limited.

Third, and ironically, funders and recipient governments, though generally considered partners in the official aid world, are only weakly accountable to one another.
Recipients regularly criticize funders for being inflexible, unresponsive, and unpredictable. Funders, for their part, criticize recipients for a lack of transparency and a
failure to fulfill obligations. These problems are only exacerbated by an increase in the
number of funders and by their different budget cycles and reporting requirements.
Because the recipient's accountability to any single funder is diluted, transaction costs
rise, as does the administrative burden on recipient governments.

Accountability is only one of the enduring challenges of foreign aid. Another is
the divergence between objectives of funders and recipients. For any particular grant
or aid transfer, the funder and the recipient may not agree fully on the objective.
They may both want to see more children learn more in school, for example—but
the funder may also want to procure a textbook contract for the home country (an
input), provide consultancies (another input), or simply buy the allegiance of a recipient government to its broader foreign policy goals. The recipient government, in turn,
may place a high priority on creating jobs (through school construction) or mollifying
the teachers' union (by allowing paid double shifts), independent of any tradeoff with
maximizing what children learn.

Beyond challenges of accountability and divergent objectives, another stumbling
block is asymmetric information. Even when there is reasonably good alignment
of funder and recipient objectives, the funder and recipient may not have the same
information or the same perspective on what might be called the local production
function—the mix of inputs in a particular setting that buys the best and greatest outcome at the lowest cost. Continuing the education example, the funder may believe

> **And ironically, funders and recipient governments are only weakly accountable to one another**

the right inputs are those for improving the quality rather than expanding the quantity of current education, or the funder may be committed to decentralization as a key strategy. Such commitments may follow either from the funder's direct experience elsewhere or from the funder's reading of the current views of international experts. The recipient government, by contrast, may be convinced that the long-run low-cost path to increasing learning in its country is to maximize enrollment, even at some cost to quality in the short run.

Compounding the lack of shared information about what is likely to work at the start of a new program is the asymmetry that tends to accumulate once a program is implemented. No matter how much attention the funder pays to monitoring the cost and allocation of the inputs it is financing, the funder is likely to have less information about exactly how those inputs are being combined with other inputs provided by the country and translated (or not) into the desired outcomes.

The combination of overlapping but divergent objectives with unshared and asymmetric information, particularly in a context of insufficient accountability, has produced the problematic relationship between funders and recipients at the heart of the many apparent failures of aid programs.

The principal-agent problem in foreign aid

Despite some shared overarching goals, funders and recipients may work at cross purposes when their interests do not align and they have different access to information. In such circumstances, generating mutually beneficial outcomes is difficult. Economists have developed principal-agent models to study such dilemmas and explore conditions that would yield mutually beneficial outcomes.

Among the standard solutions to the principal-agent problem are cost-reimbursement and fixed-price contracts.[12] Either will motivate an agent to achieve a principal's goals. Consider when a government, the principal, hires a company, the agent, to build a road. In a cost-reimbursement approach, the government reimburses the company for the cost of building the road, perhaps with an added margin for normal profits. With a fixed-price contract, by contrast, the government pays the company an agreed amount for delivering a completed road, regardless of its cost. Under the cost-reimbursement contract, the government assumes all the risks of potential cost overruns, and the company has little incentive to save money. Under the fixed-price contract, the company assumes all risks for cost overruns and is paid only if it completes the work.

Foreign aid has traditionally used the cost-reimbursement approach, particularly when specific investment projects are involved. Funders have assumed the risk; recipients have had little incentive to contain costs. In recent decades, aid agencies have tried to shift toward fixed-price contracts in the form of policy-based loans with conditionality from the World Bank and the International Monetary Fund or as budget support from bilateral agencies. In theory, recipients must achieve certain goals for funders to disburse the money.

> **Funders and recipients both have strong political pressures to disburse aid payments**

The traditional cost-reimbursement mindset, in particular, has led funders and recipients into two patterns that consistently keep them from efficiently achieving their aims. In one pattern, funders who risk cost overruns (whether the project turns out to be more expensive than originally estimated or reaches fewer beneficiaries than anticipated) seek more and more detailed information to assure themselves that the recipient government is exerting sufficient effort, implementing the right strategy, and buying inputs at the lowest cost. This not only increases costs of monitoring and administration but also implicitly demonstrates a lack of trust between the funder and recipient. Small wonder that recipients react to calls for additional reports as an unnecessary burden and even an affront.

In the second pattern, recipients who bear less risk under cost-reimbursement contracts have little incentive to use funds efficiently. Indeed, higher costs or failures to realize benefits can favor a new round of funding. Blame for failure under these contracts is hard to assign, reducing the likelihood of any consequences. Recipients can argue, often legitimately, that the funder's plan or technical support was inadequate. Funders can point to a recipient's failure to allocate enough effort to implement what was otherwise a perfect plan.

A shift toward paying fixed prices for deliverables, in the form of budget support and policy conditionality loans, has improved the situation somewhat. In these programs, funders and recipients negotiate targets, and funders agree to make payments if targets are met. However, such contracts have been undermined by a lack of clarity over targets and too great an openness to renegotiation. Since the goals of these sector and good governance programs are often broad, precise and independent measures of progress are difficult to specify. Furthermore, funders and recipients both have strong political pressures to disburse aid payments and have tended to soften conditions or offer waivers to ensure that funds are disbursed.[13]

Given the problems with fixed-price agreements, why haven't aid agencies done more to specify targets and outcomes? The most common objection is that buying development is not as easy as buying a road. Making a fixed-price contract requires specifying the service with enough precision to know when it has been delivered. Improving health, educating children, or reducing poverty seem difficult to describe as deliverable. Yet this only begs the question. If measurable products in these areas could be specified, wouldn't a fixed-price contract be worth trying?

BOX 1.2
Selected meetings and events with discussions of COD Aid

Center for Global Development. *Expert Panel Discussion.* Including Australia Aid Agency by video conference. May 25, 2007. Washington, D.C., and Canberra.

Center for Global Development. *Policy-Maker Workshop on Progress-Based Aid.* October 2007. Washington, D.C.

Fast Track Initiative Meeting. December 9–11, 2007, Dakar.

Center for Global Development. *Workshop on Progress-Based Aid.* February 19–20, 2008. Washington, D.C.

Mexican Ministry of Education and Mexicanos Primeros. *Apoyo Basado en Resultados—Cash on Delivery Aid workshop.* March 11–12, 2008. Mexico City.

Education for All—Fast Track Initiative Technical Meeting. *Mobilizing Additional Resources for Education.* April 24, 2008. Tokyo.

Center for Global Development. *Peer Review of the Preliminary Cash on Delivery Aid Manuscript.* September 17, 2008. Washington, D.C.

Bill and Melinda Gates Foundation. *Video Conference on Cash on Delivery Aid and Its Application to Health.* September 18, 2008. Washington, D.C., and Seattle.

Hemispheric Think Tank Working Group. September 22, 2008. Ottawa.

Tanzanian president and delegation. September 27, 2008. Washington, D.C.

Global Partnership on Output Based Aid. September 29, 2008. Washington, D.C.

Swedish state secretary and delegation. October 9, 2008. Washington, D.C.

World Bank Operations Policy and Country Services. October 22, 2008. Washington, D.C.

United Nations Follow-up International Conference on Financing for Development to Review the Monterrey Consensus. *Cash on Delivery Aid Roundtable Discussion.* December 2, 2008. Doha.

Hemispheric Think Tank Working Group. January 13, 2009. Washington, D.C.

Canadian International Development Agency. January 22, 2009. Ottawa.

Aid Watch. *What Would the Poor Say? Debates in Aid Evaluation.* February 6, 2009. New York City.

Johns Hopkins School of Advanced International Studies. *Development Roundtable.* February 13, 2009. Washington, D.C.

World Bank Europe and Central Asia Division. *What Does It Take to Innovate for Achieving*

A second objection is that such contracts impose the risk on recipient governments, which are, it is argued, less capable of bearing financial risk. While this may be true, the international discourse is rejecting the paternalistic notion that developing countries are better off when they implement programs designed and supported by funders. Ownership by developing countries will be fully realized, according to this perspective, only when they assume the full risks (and benefits) of their actions. It is fundamentally inconsistent to promote the idea that developing countries should have more control over their own programs and policies while purporting to protect them from bearing the risks and consequences of their decisions. And current aid modalities impose high risks on recipient governments anyway, since the funds are notoriously volatile and unpredictable.[14]

While additional objections could be discussed, suffice it to say that the fixed-price approach to solving the principal-agent problem in foreign aid merits further

BOX 1.2 (continued)
Selected meetings and events with discussions of COD Aid

Results in Europe and Central Asia? February 18, 2009. Washington, D.C.

World Bank Latin America and Caribbean Division. March 19, 2009. Washington, D.C.

World Bank Sustainable Development Network. *Results Days.* March 25, 2009. Washington, D.C.

U.S. State Department and U.S. Agency for International Development. April 16, 2009. Washington, D.C.

Global Philanthropy Forum. *Eighth Annual Conference.* April 22, 2009. Washington, D.C.

Tanzanian Development Partners. *Video Conference on Cash on Delivery Aid.* May 6, 2009. Dar es Salaam, Washington, D.C., and Addis Ababa.

United Nations Economic Commission for Africa. *Trade, Finance and Development Division Seminar on Cash on Delivery Aid.* May 2009. Addis Ababa.

Sixth Plenary Meeting of the Leading Group on Innovative Financing for Development. May 29, 2009. Paris.

The Office of Congressman Sam Farr. *Policy Discussion on Conditional Cash Transfers.* June 19, 2009. Washington, D.C.

European Commission. *Meeting of EU Member States Education Experts.* June 25, 2009. Brussels.

Liberian Education Minister. November 18, 2009. Washington, D.C.

Civil Society Forum of the World Bank and International Monetary Fund Fall Meetings. *The Aid System: Does Mutual Accountability Encourage Outcomes.* October 4, 2009. Istanbul.

Malawian Ministries of Finance and Education. October 6, 2009. Lilongwe.

Malawian Development Partners. October 9, 2009. Lilongwe.

Swedish Ministry of Foreign Affairs and Swedish International Development Cooperation Agency. October 22, 2009. Stockholm.

Liberian Planning and Economic Affairs Minister and Deputy Minister. November 18, 2009. Washington, D.C.

exploration. The approach diminishes the need to monitor inputs and focuses more on measuring outcomes. It assigns greater responsibility to recipients while increasing the accountability of both funders and recipients to their citizens.

Efforts to reform aid are clearly moving in this direction, but they remain largely limited to marginal changes in the traditional approaches.[15] Such partial reform recognizes the need to give recipient countries more responsibility for their programs, encourage innovation and learning, simplify the engagement between funders and recipients, and increase accountability by focusing on outcomes, but it continues to pay more attention to getting the right plan and implementation strategy than to getting the right measures of progress, the right incentives, and the right distributions of responsibilities.

More thorough reform is needed; this book presents one possible approach. Our proposal, COD Aid, has been developed, critiqued, and improved in a comprehensive process of research and consultation. We undertook new research, commissioned background papers from experts, interviewed dozens of practitioners, and engaged

in extensive consultations with officials, technical experts, and civil society representatives to further assess and refine the idea. We also convened meetings to discuss
COD Aid and made presentations and responded to comments at events sponsored by
others. (A list of meetings and events is included in box 1.2). This book presents the
results of that work.

The next chapter describes the key features of COD Aid and discusses how it
helps funders and recipients tackle the fundamental challenges to making aid work:
accountability problems; divergent objectives; and poor and unshared information
about what works.

Notes

1.   Official aid includes aid from governments (bilateral aid) and aid financed or provided by
     UN agencies, the European Union, and multilateral development banks.

2.   Rough estimates of the cost of meeting the Millennium Development Goals beyond what
     aid-recipient countries could finance were on the order of $50 billion a year in 2000
     (Levine, Birdsall, and Ibrahim 2003). The Commission on Africa, chaired by U.K. Prime
     Minister Tony Blair, recommended in 2005 that donors double their annual aid to Africa
     by 2010 (Commission for Africa 2005).

3.   For criticism of foreign aid, see Birdsall (2008); Easterly (2006); Hausmann and Rodrik
     (2002); Moss, Pettersson, and van de Walle (2006); and Rajan and Subramanian (2005).

4.   On why impact evaluation has been uncommon, see Savedoff, Levine, and Birdsall
     (2006). Birdsall (2008) cites limited evaluation as one of funders' seven deadly sins. See
     also Pritchett (2002) on incentives not to evaluate.

5.   In most cases, countries continued to receive loans and grants whether they were fulfilling
     conditions or not (Birdsall, Claessens, and Diwan 2003).

6.   Chang 2005.

7.   World Bank (2004) evaluates progress in the implementation of Poverty Reduction Strat-
     egy Papers. Studies that question the effectiveness of Poverty Reduction Strategy Papers
     (PRSPs) and the quality of participation include Birdsall (2008), Christian Aid (2001,
     2002), Easterly (2006), and Ranis (2008). Ranis (2008) reports that at a Kampala meet-
     ing "fifteen African countries denounced the PRSPs as structural adjustment loans in
     sheep's clothing."

8.   Birdsall (2007) refers to this as the problem of exit. Selowsky (2003) also documents the
     tendency to waive conditions on adjustment loans, which are essentially predecessors of
     budget support.

9.   This is often the case for fragile states. For a definition of fragile states, see OECD (2006).
     For information on the limitation of aid to these types of states, see Development Assis-
     tance Committee (2008a); Fritz and Menocal (2007); Grindle (2007); Cammack (2007);
     and Randall (2007).

10. Development Assistance Committee 2008b.

11. These problems can exist in any type of transfer, including one from central to local governments. See chapter 6.
12. See, for example, Milgrom and Roberts (1992).
13. Killick 1998; Devarajan, Dollar, and Holmgren 2001; Easterly 2002.
14. Kharas 2008.
15. For example, in the Accra Agenda for Action (an agreement ratified by the delegates to the Third High Level Forum on Aid Effectiveness in Accra, Ghana, in September 2008) funders called for more transparency but created no new incentives for it.

A solution:
Cash on Delivery Aid

Cash on Delivery Aid (COD Aid) is a funding mechanism designed to address and overcome the drawbacks of foreign aid identified in the preceding chapter. While many previous efforts to reform foreign aid have pursued limited improvements, COD Aid is meant to be a more thorough approach to altering funder-recipient relationships, providing new means to ensure accountability and achieve shared goals.

The core of COD Aid is a contract for funders and recipients to agree on a mutually desired outcome and a fixed payment for each unit of confirmed progress (box 2.1). This chapter delineates the key features of COD Aid and the basic steps in fulfilling the contract. It next explores the advantages of COD Aid, both in correcting the evident shortcomings of earlier aid and in achieving the newly articulated goals for future aid. As a substantial departure from previous aid practices, COD Aid naturally raises legitimate reservations and concerns. This chapter responds to the concerns that were raised in our extensive consultations. The chapter then compares COD Aid and other results-based approaches to aid, clarifying how it is distinguished from and builds on these other approaches.

The COD Aid principles can be used for transfers between a variety of actors, such as between private philanthropic foundations and governments or between central and lower levels of government (chapter 6). The basic design can also be applied in any sector where an appropriate outcome measure can be identified. In chapter 3, we provide extensive details on its application to universal primary schooling. Further examples are discussed in chapter 7, including preventing the spread of HIV/AIDS, increasing household consumption of potable water, reducing carbon emissions, improving domestic statistical systems, and increasing citizen use of public data as a way to promote transparency and democracy.

BOX 2.1
Basics of COD Aid

Key features
- Payment for outcomes, not inputs
- Hands-off funders, responsible recipients
- Independent verification
- Transparency through public dissemination
- Complementarity with other aid programs

Basic steps
- Two parties negotiate and sign a medium-term (for example, five-year) contract
- Recipient government pursues its own strategy
- Recipient government collects and reports data (for example, annually)
- Funder arranges independent audit (for example, annually)
- Funder makes payment for confirmed results (for example, annually)
- Third party finances research (optional)

Advantages
- Accountability
- Local ownership and institutions
- Learning by doing
- Workable in most low-income developing countries
- Opportunities to attract private funders
- Progress toward the 2005 Paris Declaration

Risks and concerns
- Displacement of other aid programs
- Too little, too late
- Unintended consequences
- Waste and corruption
- Difficulty measuring outcomes
- No progress means no payment

Although COD Aid is conceived as a substantial and fundamental change in the way some foreign aid programs are conducted, it is not intended to supplant all other forms of foreign assistance. Instead, we see COD Aid as complementing many existing foreign aid programs. Indeed, when its mechanisms for measuring progress, providing incentives, and clarifying responsibilities become established, we believe COD Aid will help funders and recipients make much more efficient use of existing resources across a spectrum of aid programs.

Key features and basic steps

COD Aid enables funders and recipients to pursue mutually desired outcomes through a contract that specifies the results that recipients will achieve and the fixed payments that funders will provide. A financial aid mechanism can be considered to be COD Aid if it has five key features.

First and most fundamental, the funder makes payments for outcomes, not inputs. The outcome (or outcomes) must be agreed between the funder and recipient. It must also be measurable and continuous (such as, number of children enrolled), making it possible to reward incremental progress. At no point does the funder specify or monitor inputs. There are no required policies, training programs, or outside consultancies; no agreed contracts for building, renovating, or maintaining bricks and mortar; no specified forms of management, reforms, or decisions.

Second, the funder embraces a hands-off approach, emphasizing the power of incentives rather than guidance or interference, even with good ideas. The funder not only does not pay for inputs, but indeed entirely eschews designing or demanding any particular set of inputs. A funder may make available or help obtain other resources for technical assistance, ideally in a pooled fund. But it is up to the recipient to choose whether to contract for technical help and advice from any party, including that from funders.[1]

Conversely, where the funder is hands-off, the recipient has complete discretion and responsibility. This extends from the initial design and planning right through to the implementation of strategies. All decisions and plans, including whether to have a plan, are up to the recipient government. Further, the funds a recipient receives after making progress can be used in any way, determined by the recipient: to reduce the fiscal deficit, pay off debt, build roads, finance increased health services—or in education to train teachers, subsidize school meals, pay cash to households that keep their children in school, provide prize grants to districts whose schools perform well or compensation grants to poorer districts. In short, without funder-imposed conditions or restrictions on the use of funds, COD Aid permits and requires recipients to assume full responsibility for progressing toward agreed goals.

Third, progress toward the agreed outcome is independently verified by a third party (neither funder nor recipient). Progress is the trigger for COD Aid payments. So, both funder and recipient must have confidence in the way progress is measured. Independent verification should take the form of a financial and performance audit, with no restrictions on the nationality or other characteristics of the auditing firm. Audits are paid for by the funder (see chapter 4 for more on audits). Once progress is verified, the funder pays for the improved outcomes. The information about outcomes is a further significant benefit of COD Aid.

Fourth is transparency, achieved by publicly disseminating the content of the COD Aid contract itself, the amount of progress, and the payment for each increment of progress. To encourage public scrutiny and understanding, the indicator or measure of progress should be as simple as possible. Simplicity and transparency increase the credibility of the arrangement, help ensure that the parties fulfill their commitments, improve accountability to the public, and encourage broader social engagement in aspects of progress beyond the specific object of the contract. In the education example in chapter 3, we note that the results of any testing should also be publicly disseminated.

Fifth, COD Aid complements other aid programs. We believe that COD Aid can and should be introduced as additional to current aid flows in a particular recipient country without disrupting ongoing programs. Indeed, we argue that COD Aid would create healthy incentives for more efficient use of existing resources by both funders and recipients.

COD Aid enables funders and recipients to pursue mutually desired outcomes

After confirming outcomes, the funder pays the agreed amount per unit of progress

How would these five features be implemented? In practical terms, in a COD Aid project funders and recipients would take the following steps:

The first is for the funder and recipient to negotiate and sign a contract. Elements of the contract to be negotiated include the measure of progress, the amount of payment for progress, the length of the agreement's term and a list of mutually agreed auditors (a sample funder-recipient contract is in the appendix). We suggest a minimum contract period of five years. This would give the recipient time to plan, execute, evaluate, and adjust the strategy for making progress. Adjustments here are understood to comprise not merely adding or switching inputs but also engaging in political and institutional change.

The second step is for the recipient to take action to progress toward the agreed goal. Because COD Aid follows a hands-off approach, the recipient has full discretion over how to achieve progress. The funder may make technical assistance available, directly or through a pooled fund, but has no further involvement in design, strategy, inputs, or implementation. The recipient defines and pursues the route to progress.

The third step is for the recipient to measure outcomes and make the collected data public. Relevant data to be collected will already have been determined in the initial contract negotiations. The direct costs of data collection, analysis, and publication may be covered by funders (such a provision is included in the model contract in the appendix).

The fourth crucial step in COD Aid is an independent audit. The funder hires an auditor from the preapproved list of mutually acceptable auditors. The auditor verifies the recipient's report of outcomes (see the sample funder-auditor contract in the appendix).

Only when the first four steps are completed does the fifth step, payment, occur. After confirming outcomes, the funder pays the agreed amount per unit of progress in line with any provisions in the contract for differences between the auditor's and recipient's reports. Payments are unconditional transfers to the recipient.

In a five-year contract, steps three, four, and five would be repeated annually.

A further optional step is systematic research on the response of both funders and recipients to implementing COD Aid in a particular setting. As outlined in chapter 5, the benefits of such research would accrue largely, but not only, to the funders and recipients directly involved. Others would also learn from and could exploit the documented experiences. This further research is a highly desirable but optional step, appropriately financed in part or in full by a third party. If this research is financed, the recipient government should be obligated in the initial funder-recipient contract to provide information and make staff and citizens available for surveys and other data collection.

Advantages of COD Aid: why it could succeed where other approaches fail

An aid program embodying these key features and steps would, we believe, bring many advantages to the global system of foreign aid. In designing COD Aid, we have studied the shortcomings of the traditional system, the limitations of previous efforts at reform, the unmet needs and disappointments of various stakeholders, and the goals articulated in the 2005 Paris Declaration. We have devised an approach that we believe will foster accountability, build local ownership, permit learning by doing, and work even in fragile states—while also attracting new private funders, enabling funder coordination, reducing administrative burdens, and facilitating the expansion of aid.

Accountability among funders, recipients, and their constituents

COD Aid could have a major impact on one of the most enduring problems of foreign aid transfers: accountability. As noted in chapter 1, aid as practiced does not instill accountability between the funder government and its citizens, the recipient government and its citizens, or between the funder and recipient governments. COD Aid—with its focus on outcomes, independent verification, transparency, and recipient discretion and responsibility—could generate an entirely different framework for the many actors in foreign aid to demand and ensure accountability to each other.

First, COD Aid makes funders more accountable to their citizens by linking foreign assistance to specific outcomes. Because cash is disbursed only after progress is achieved, funders can present information on outcomes to constituents, showing that foreign aid is effective. We believe that taxpayers want aid to buy results, and COD Aid helps funders make clear statements, such as "Our funds paid for 1,000 more children to finish school." Particularly for funders who view general budget support to developing countries skeptically, COD Aid provides the explicit link to outcomes that may allow them, in exchange, to offer recipients more flexibility and autonomy in the use of funds.

Second, COD Aid makes recipient governments more accountable to their citizens. Because it requires transparency, particularly by requiring that outcome measures be publicly reported, citizens and civil society groups will have information on progress that is not available in most countries. For education, nongovernmental organizations (NGOs) might use this information to hold governments to account in many ways. Creating school report cards, for example, has increased civic engagement with schools and improved quality in many settings.[2] The funder's financing commitment is also public, making it possible for citizens to better assess their government's claims of financial constraints.

> COD Aid provides recipients more flexibility and autonomy in the use of funds

Third, COD Aid improves mutual accountability between funders and recipients because the contracts are less ambiguous—focusing on shared goals and measured outcomes rather than on differences over strategy or expenditure tracking. In this way, COD Aid avoids the too-frequent practice of renegotiating after the fact whether particular expenses were allowed, bidding procedures acceptable, or targets adequately met under sector programs. Less ambiguity also makes funding more predictable, a key concern regularly raised by recipient governments when they denounce unpredictable aid flows as a problem for planning and management. With COD Aid, payments are as predictable as the government's projections of its own likelihood of progress.

In one respect, COD Aid would seem to reduce accountability: funders do not monitor and control the way recipients spend COD Aid funds. Yet the traditional forms of micromanagement that track spending give only an illusion of control. They allow funders to count how many books or hours of training were purchased with their funds and from whom, but not whether the books were actually used or kept behind the teacher's desk to avoid damage, whether training was useful or quickly forgotten. Even when properly collected, such information is not genuinely useful for policy decisions. And it imposes a substantial administrative burden on recipients. In contrast, the data required in a COD Aid agreement focus on outcomes rather than inputs—central for both policymaking and accountability. That is why the first key feature of COD Aid, the focus on outcomes rather than inputs, is so important.

Local ownership and institutions: recipient responsibility and discretion

The 2005 Paris Declaration is only one of the more prominent public statements to affirm that aid is more effective when developing country governments have full responsibility for their own policies and programs—that is, local ownership. Traditional approaches to aid have had considerable difficulty in realizing this aim; recent efforts such as budget support and the contracts under the U.S. Millennium Challenge Account do somewhat better. COD Aid takes a further step toward promoting recipient responsibility and discretion. The payments through COD Aid are not restricted ex ante for any particular use (though with more accountability). They are not conditional on the country's economic policies or education policies (curricular reform). Nor are they tied to particular inputs (teacher training or textbooks) or intermediate outputs (number of schools built).

> With COD Aid, payments are as predictable as the government's projections of its own likelihood of progress

The payments go to the recipient and then to whatever institutions (public or private schools, school districts, NGOs, subnational governments, families) or other purposes (health, agriculture, deficit reduction) the recipient chooses. The funder does not specify that funds go to a particular ministry, special implementing unit, contracted consulting firm, or NGO, as is now common. COD Aid thus puts resources and responsibility in recipient hands. It gives recipients the flexibility and freedom to conduct their own diagnostic studies, develop their own strategies, seek technical support at their discretion, experiment with new approaches, take credit for successes, and assume responsibility for failures. This level of recipient responsibility generates five further benefits.

COD Aid puts resources and responsibility in recipient hands

COD Aid encourages institution-building. In many countries, aid programs bypass normal government planning. Money may go to projects managed outside the government budget, unbeknownst to the finance, education, or other ministries. Aid programs are particularly apt to create such parallel mechanisms in countries with lower incomes or weaker institutions. The funder's involvement in designing and implementing programs can thus undermine the government's decisionmaking for allocating funds, a process central to democratic governance. And while the funder's involvement in all stages of the program may ensure a degree of technical support and continuity, it also removes incentives and opportunities for the recipient to build its own capacities to design, implement, and manage programs in the long run (figure 2.1).

Aid programs with extensive funder involvement can also divert government attention from the need for institutional development and toward managing foreign aid. In some cases, funder micromanagement might effectively buy AIDS drugs or train teachers but do little to ensure that recipients will have the capacity to deliver health care or education in the long run. So, even in the world's most fragile states, COD Aid could make a particularly positive contribution.

To build local capacity, funders have agreed that recipient governments should be more involved in deciding how aid funds are spent and that more aid should flow through recipient country budget systems.[3] Progress in making these two aims a reality has been mixed. COD Aid would make both happen automatically.

FIGURE 2.1
COD Aid changes the roles of funders and recipients

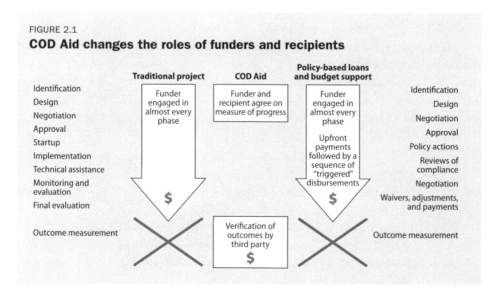

Recipients are free to test strategies and choose the most effective ones

COD Aid gives recipients more discretion to address binding constraints in whatever sector. Since payments are not tied to particular inputs, recipients are free to test strategies and choose the most effective ones, regardless of sector. For example, if COD Aid were applied to a primary education initiative, the funds would not necessarily have to be used by the ministry of education. Instead, funds might increase demand through conditional cash transfers or school feeding programs. If the recipient views labor relations as a key issue, funds could be used to change the dynamics of negotiations with unions—for example, financing incentives for teachers to work in rural areas or establishing programs to encourage early retirement of unqualified teachers. Funds might even fix impassable roads in districts where transportation problems limit attendance—or speed disbursements to purchase teaching supplies.

Technical assistance is demand-driven. In traditional aid programs, funders often provide technical assistance for designing and implementing programs regardless of whether they have the most relevant expertise. This is particularly problematic when funders push ideas that are fashionable in international debates but that may not be relevant to a particular setting.[4] With COD Aid, recipients can use local knowledge of problems to assess which kinds of technical assistance from which sources will be most relevant. Such demand-driven technical assistance has a greater chance of being useful to recipients, and because they selected it, they are more likely to apply it.

Recipient responsibility also fosters local involvement and accountability. Over time, both funders and recipients have become dissatisfied with approaches that treat beneficiaries as objects rather than subjects of their own development. While progress has been made through greater consultation (surveys and focus groups) and participation (community meetings, design workshops, and demand-driven programs), these processes were largely instigated by the funder's agenda (developing a poverty reduction strategy).[5] With COD Aid, recipients can develop their strategies through local debate and existing channels for accountability to citizens. With the public fully informed of the amount of COD Aid at stake, accountability can be strengthened in ways that fit domestic political dynamics.

Increased discretion gives recipients the freedom to engage with private and nonprofit initiatives. Once the funder cedes responsibility to the recipient, it is easier to include nontraditional actors. The COD Aid agreement gives the recipient an incentive to achieve goals by any means, including collaborations, partnerships, or contracts with private or nonprofit organizations. For example, national leaders might respond to a COD Aid agreement that seeks to increase primary school completion by simplifying regulatory restrictions on private schools or by establishing a voucher program. Under an agreement to reduce the prevalence of tuberculosis, national leaders might contract with private healthcare providers or pharmacies.[6] This flexibility would be particularly welcome where nonprofit and even commercial firms provide a significant share of services used by the poor.[7]

Learning by doing: COD Aid fosters experimentation and assessment

Without information about whether goals are being met, it is difficult to determine whether programs are successful. Yet current aid provides weak incentives to get reliable information about outcomes. With COD Aid, those incentives are strong.

Both funders and recipients have strong incentives to invest in collecting good data on outcomes. Recipients want information on outcomes because it triggers aid payments; funders want the information to be assured that they are paying for real progress. In traditional aid, recipients are rewarded mostly for documenting their expenditures and reporting on procurement, while funders consider their funds well spent if they can show how many inputs were purchased.

COD Aid encourages learning by doing. Collecting information on outcomes is not an end in itself. By measuring progress, COD Aid establishes ideal conditions for learning by doing. It gives recipients discretion, permitting experimentation and innovation, and requires measurement of outcomes, making it possible to assess which of those experiments and innovations are most promising. In this way, funders and recipients learn about the effectiveness of a range of policies and programs and build knowledge about which ones work and which ones don't. (Chapter 5 discusses in detail how a research program could complement a government's own accumulation of learning.)

COD Aid can work in most low-income developing countries—even in fragile states

Another advantage of COD Aid is that it can work almost anywhere. The challenges of implementation and the likelihood of success will vary with context. The main characteristic of a country where COD Aid could make a big difference is one where the promise of additional unconstrained funds could facilitate effective action to achieve shared development goals. Other contextual factors—the amount of money, the potential gains, the information systems, the institutional capacity—only make the likelihood of success greater or smaller.

At least 40 countries receive more than 10 percent of their GDP in aid,[8] many of them viewed as fragile states.[9] In fragile states, encouraging development through foreign aid is extremely difficult, regardless of its form. The key challenges to implementing COD Aid in such countries are:

COD Aid can work almost anywhere

- Establishing a baseline for measuring progress.

- Verifying progress when information systems are weak.
- Relying on the government to design new strategies and articulate demand for technical assistance.
- Relying on the government to implement its program with a weak institutional base.
- Expecting the political system to respond coherently to the externally generated incentives.

COD Aid might be more successful in fragile states than traditional forms of aid for three reasons. First, because COD Aid requires verified progress to trigger payment, it requires serious efforts to gather data and establish information systems, which can make a large difference for subsequent policymaking. All too often, this core requirement of good governance is addressed only after meeting more immediate needs, even when it is unclear whether ongoing actions are making any difference. Second, while it may be risky to rely on governments in fragile states to design and implement their own programs, traditional approaches that substitute foreign for domestic institutional capacity only maintain dependence and compromise sustainability. Third, fragile states may have more flexibility to respond to COD Aid's incentives with innovative approaches because vested interests are weaker and government bureaucracies less entrenched and less resistant to innovations.

COD Aid may be particularly relevant for fragile states with new and effective leaders. Currently, such countries may not have access to aid that requires demonstrations of good governance. For example, a country that has recently emerged from a civil war may not be eligible for budget support if its public financial management is poor. Yet it could sign a forward-looking COD Aid agreement and begin to reap the benefits of its success in achieving social goals in a fairly short time.

At the other end of the spectrum, COD Aid may seem irrelevant to large countries with strong domestic capacity for public policy. But COD Aid funds are additional and unconstrained. So, even if the amounts are small, COD Aid might offer these governments a new resource or lever for introducing change in contexts where there are strong vested interests and entrenched bureaucracies that might hamper experimentation. Or, national governments might be interested in using the COD Aid to encourage progress in worse off regions, particularly if they have a federal political structure.

In general, the benefits of COD Aid are probably greatest in poorer and more aid-dependent countries. COD Aid might be easier to implement in a country with better data and a more organized and capable government bureaucracy, but the gains might be greatest where data are poor (because COD Aid generates incentives for government to establish management information systems) and where bureaucracies are hide-bound and inflexible (because COD Aid provides incentives that might unlock creative solutions even in a difficult environment).

> **COD Aid might be more successful in fragile states than traditional forms of aid**

COD Aid creates opportunities to attract private funders

Attracting private funders to foreign aid is another major advantage. Some private funders—whether corporations, foundations, privately funded NGOs, or individuals—continue to finance traditional projects. But many have become aware that their efforts are small relative to the gains that could be made if public policy were to improve. In addition, as the scale of private philanthropy has increased, many of the same issues facing public donors have arisen. One school might be built without coordinating with the government, but not a hundred. Sometimes private funders are too small to engage in meaningful sectorwide policy discussions. And in many cases, private funders are cautious about moving into broader sector debates because they cannot envision grants for such intangibles as policy reform.

COD Aid makes it easy to reach out and include such funders in two ways: it reduces the administrative costs of engaging in coordinated funder action, and it links payments to specific measurable outcomes. The funder's ability to report on the outcomes it has paid for is particularly useful in relating to its constituents (shareholders, managers, members, or contributors).

The 2005 Paris Declaration and aid effectiveness: from rhetoric to real reform

Another advantage is that COD Aid will help funders fulfill the commitments made in the 2005 Paris Declaration—for local ownership, coordination, harmonization, outcome focus, and accountability by establishing an explicit and publicly visible contractual arrangement. COD Aid ensures that funds flow to pursue the shared goal (more students completing school) while aligning with the recipient's own policies, programs, and strategies.

COD Aid also provides useful discipline for funders. Once the contract is signed, the funder cannot indulge the temptation to direct funds toward parallel executing units and pet projects, toward its own preferred form of technical assistance and suppliers, or even to alternative or changing objectives (such as geopolitical aims or pleasing particular domestic constituencies). The potential of COD Aid for aid effectiveness as envisioned in the 2005 Paris Declaration has several parts.

COD Aid coordinates actions of official funders. Once a COD Aid agreement is in place, any number of funders can join the program without increasing administrative or coordination costs. The goal is explicit and shared; the reporting requirements and outcome measures are uniform; a single mechanism exists for auditing and verifying reported progress. Additional funds can be added either to increase the size of the incentive for each unit of progress (additional child who completes primary school) or to extend the agreement to additional countries, without increasing the program's

COD Aid will help funders fulfill the commitments in the 2005 Paris Declaration

complexity. COD Aid is also perfectly suited to disbursing a pool of funds through a single payment mechanism, though that is not necessary. This would go even further in ensuring funder coordination and reducing the administrative burden on recipient countries (box 2.2). And it would facilitate contributions from private philanthropies.

If such a pooled fund were created through a global compact, the price list or fixed payment for each measure of progress could be the same for all countries. The payments would then be correspondingly more valuable in less developed countries, where wages and costs are typically lower. And because it is generally easier and cheaper to improve from a low base than from a higher one (expanding primary completion when the baseline is only 60 percent compared with 90 percent), the payment would

---

BOX 2.2
Should COD Aid be negotiated for each country or established as a global compact?

In developing the concept for COD Aid, we debated whether COD Aid should be tailored to each country or negotiated as a global compact for countries to join voluntarily.

In the first case, one or more funders would negotiate COD Aid contracts with a recipient country. This approach allows funders and recipients to adjust agreements to different goals, measures, and forms of verification. The deliberative process of choosing a measure of progress might be, in itself, beneficial to public policy formation.

But, we conclude that a global compact offers substantial benefits to funders and recipients that a country-by-country approach cannot match.[1] With a global compact, a group of funders and recipient countries would collectively design a COD Aid agreement. Once it became operational, funders would commit funds according to the agreement, and eligible recipient countries would choose whether to take advantage of the agreement.

Administrative costs would be substantially reduced by collectively negotiating the COD Aid agreement just once. With the COD Aid compact in place, funders of any kind (public or private, large or small) could commit funds to a common pool or to specific recipients but always according to the same criteria. For education, this would mean the agreements would all use the same definition of completion, the same process for approving tests, the same process and agents for verifying and auditing outcomes. A single global compact would ensure harmonization and coordination among funders and limit opportunities for manipulating agreements to favor the interests of a particular funder or recipient.

A standard contract would also promote fairness and transparency. By setting a uniform payment, it would ensure that lives and beneficiaries are not valued more in one country than another. Such uniformity would also assist civil society and others in interpreting whether the agreements are being implemented and whether their countries are performing well relative to others.

Some practical issues would arise in establishing a global compact, but they are manageable. For example, it may be necessary for the compact to specify eligibility standards (such as the country's income or governance score) or to offer a limited set of progress measures that would be feasible in different contexts.

Note
1. Barder and Birdsall's (2006) original description of COD Aid (as "payments for progress") was as a single offer by one or more funders to any partner (recipient) country.

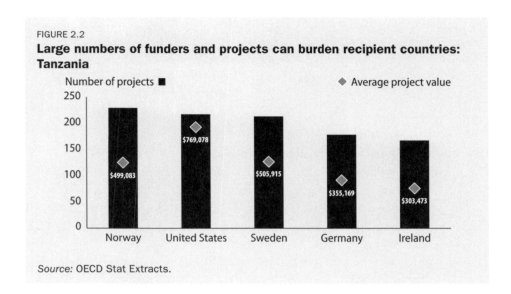

FIGURE 2.2

Large numbers of funders and projects can burden recipient countries: Tanzania

Number of projects ■   ◆ Average project value

Source: OECD Stat Extracts.

be more valuable for countries that are currently further behind. Governments that find ways to provide services at lower cost would benefit from the resulting surplus, acting as an incentive to use public funds efficiently.

COD Aid reduces the administrative burden on recipient governments—and on funders too. When dozens of funders operate in the same country, they create large administrative costs (figure 2.2). Funders that take the 2005 Paris Declaration seriously need to spend much time and effort to coordinate among themselves. Recipient governments are also burdened with meetings and managing independent arrangements with many foreign agencies. In fact, officials' time in aid-dependent countries is often occupied extensively by meeting and coordinating with funders (see box 1.1). By reducing the burden of administration, COD Aid might be even more appropriate for weak and fragile states, which could focus on executing their own programs and measuring outcomes.

COD aid complements budget support, project aid, and traditional technical assistance. COD Aid creates incentives for the recipient government to maximize, however it can, the effectiveness of its programs and of its support from funders. Indeed, with COD Aid, governments need not spend more money; they have an incentive to do more with resources they have. Most governments are well within the frontier that defines effective use of resources for public services.

COD Aid facilitates scaling up foreign aid. In the last decades, funders have harnessed political support to obtain substantial funds for foreign aid. Yet negotiating traditional aid projects is labor intensive, and arranging for the expansion of sector programs takes time. By contrast, negotiating new COD Aid programs is fairly quick and can channel as much funding as can be mobilized. Once COD Aid agreements are in place, funders could apply additional funds by increasing the size of the incentives or expanding the number of countries that are eligible, with minimal demands on technical or administrative staff.

Concerns and risks—and how to manage them

COD Aims to fundamentally change the way foreign aid operates, in the funder-recipient relationship and in the assignment of accountability, responsibility, and focus of aid programs. Its key features—payment for outcome, hands-off funders and responsible recipients, independent verification, transparency, and complementarity—chart a new path for foreign assistance. We have laid out the manifold advantages we believe this new approach to foreign aid will provide. We also know the risks in embarking on this new path. Indeed, careful attention to the legitimate and reasonable concerns expressed in various consultations and meetings have influenced the design and enabled us to refine and improve the COD Aid proposal.

Some risks specific to COD Aid can be contained during negotiations by carefully defining the agreed measure of progress, explicitly specifying financial arrangements (such as escrow accounts), or providing for third-party verification. Other risks, such as diversions of funds, are common to all forms of aid. In most cases, these common risks may actually be better managed through the structure of a COD Aid agreement. The most serious and frequently raised concerns about COD Aid are shared and responded to here.

Displacement of other aid programs?

In our consultations, representatives from funding agencies and recipient governments were concerned that COD Aid would substitute for existing foreign aid approaches. While this is possible, it is neither likely nor advisable in the short to medium term. Displacing other aid programs is unlikely because agencies and governments already have contractual arrangements in place for multiyear programs. Since COD Aid is not paid until progress is achieved, the funding through existing aid channels may be an important resource that would permit recipients to respond effectively to the COD Aid incentive. Furthermore, it would be inadvisable to replace existing aid modalities with COD Aid until the new approach is tried and tested. For these reasons, we propose (and discuss in chapter 4) that funders commit to making COD Aid additional to their current and projected commitments. This commitment would apply, at a minimum, through the term of the contract, which we propose to be five years, with the possibility of a five-year extension.

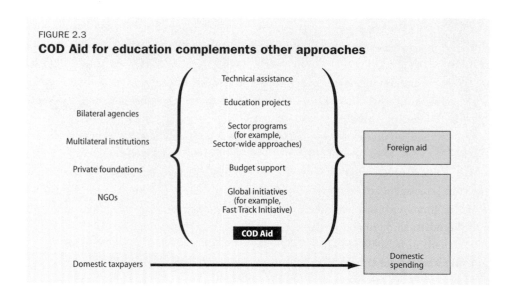

FIGURE 2.3
COD Aid for education complements other approaches

Bilateral agencies

Multilateral institutions

Private foundations

NGOs

Domestic taxpayers

Technical assistance

Education projects

Sector programs
(for example,
Sector-wide approaches)

Budget support

Global initiatives
(for example,
Fast Track Initiative)

COD Aid

Foreign aid

Domestic
spending

Too little, too late?

COD Aid is paid when recipients achieve outcomes, not when a government initiates reforms or new programs. In our consultations, participants expressed the concern that countries will not be able to reach the initiative's goals without funds for initial investments. By definition, COD Aid cannot provide this support upfront without undercutting its emphasis on outcomes. But this does not mean that countries will be without resources for meeting goals. COD Aid would be only one source within the envelope of foreign aid and domestic spending (for education, see figure 2.3). In countries heavily dependent on outside resources, existing aid flows are likely to matter for any efforts to accelerate progress under a COD Aid agreement at least in the first year before the COD Aid begins to flow. This is true for real investments (building schools, distributing textbooks, reforming curricula) and for technical assistance that a recipient might request.

The question is whether COD Aid payments present a sufficient incentive to spur funders and recipients to search farther afield for efficiencies in the use of current resources. Because education outcomes in developing countries have only a weak relationship to public spending, we believe there is some scope for greater efficiency in some countries, if not all. Furthermore, existing aid flows and aid-financed programs (including budget support) are likely to be a good source of funding for a government to implement reforms or try pilot programs to increase enrollment and raise quality in education.

Governments with a COD Aid contract might be in a good position to raise matching private money or even to borrow against expected future

> COD Aid would be only one source within the envelope of foreign aid and domestic spending

An inappropriate outcome measure could lead to unintended consequences

COD Aid payments to finance upfront investments.[10] Funders might also respond with financing innovations, as in health.[11] In short, we believe COD Aid will encourage better use of existing resources, public and private, domestic and foreign. We also want to underscore that COD Aid should be additional to existing aid. Indeed, at least for the initial five-year contract, this addition is critical.

A single exception exists to COD Aid's exclusion of upfront funding: reimbursement for the cost of creating a system to gather reliable information on outcomes. For example, for an agreement in which funders commit to pay a fixed sum for each additional student who takes a test in the final year of primary school, the initial costs for developing and applying the test could be financed by funders (see chapter 3 and the appendix for more details).

Unintended consequences?

One hazard of COD Aid is that an inappropriate outcome measure could lead to unintended consequences. Domestic resources might be diverted to one sector and away from others. For example, if the COD Aid agreement pays for expanding primary completion, funds might be diverted from other priorities such as improving health or rural infrastructure, although the overall social return might be higher in these sectors.

This concern can be mitigated to some extent by the size of the payment. If the payment is large enough to cover the cost of progress (such as the marginal cost of ensuring an additional child completes primary school), funding for other priorities would not be affected. With a smaller payment, diversion of resources is an issue that funders and recipient countries would have to consider seriously. If the COD Aid approach were successful in one area, funders could offer a range of contracts to cover the spectrum of development objectives that they share with developing countries.

For education, an immediate concern is that a country that is paid for the quantity of children who complete school might expand enrollment at the expense of schooling quality. One response to this risk is to identify a measure of progress that closely approximates the shared goal and minimizes such foreseeable problems. This could involve finding an outcome measure that relates to learning and not just school attendance. Another response is to mobilize social groups that can monitor aspects of the program that are not easily measured. Again, for education, this might include providing parents, political parties, and civic organizations with access to school information such as the results of student literacy tests, school budgets, and test results.

In our consultations, we also heard concerns that recipients might direct funding to better-off areas where it is easier to make progress or to better-off groups who are easier to reach, perhaps ignoring children who are socially excluded, from ethnic minorities, or living with disabilities. The tradeoffs in choosing where to expand public services and for whom cannot be avoided. For social services, some countries have expansion plans that seek to maximize the number of beneficiaries as fast as possible within their limited resources. In such cases, resources may go to relatively better-off areas where it is easier to make progress. Other countries have chosen expansion plans that seek to ensure that gains are more widely spread across geographic, gender, income, and ethnic differences, though this may come at the cost of reaching more beneficiaries. These are tradeoffs that even the richest countries face and that ultimately are resolved only through the political process, with national public debate.

Waste and corruption?

COD Aid maximizes the recipient's discretion in using funds, making it virtually impossible for funders to ensure that COD Aid payments are used only for legiti-mate public purposes. But this is fundamentally true of all foreign aid. Even the most detailed monitoring of spending on traditional development projects cannot guarantee that the recipient country is not taking advantage of the increased resources to release other funds for inappropriate uses. The risk that COD Aid might encourage waste and corruption can be mitigated by establishing standards for public financial accountabil-ity as a condition of eligibility. Or, funders can accept the risk and rely on the improved assurance that, regardless how the money is spent, progress has been achieved.

Some funders already provide aid that is delinked from specific inputs, as through budget support. These funders address corruption and financial controls through conditions for good policies or improving public financial management—or through reviews such as the World Bank's Public Expenditure Reviews and Public Expenditure and Financial Accountability reports.[12] These approaches are likely to be more helpful than the intense attention paid to tracking aid dollars and rooting out corruption just in those projects for which aid is spent. More to the point, COD funds are no more likely to be subject to corruption than other aid channeled through recipient budgets or than money freed up when funders finance specific programs or projects.

Under COD Aid, recipients receive payments for each unit of progress regardless of how it is achieved. So, another way that funds could be wasted is by rewarding recipi-ents for progress even when success is due to other causes. The only way to avoid this would be to use elaborate, expensive, and possibly intrusive methods for attributing success to specific actions by the recipient. We are not concerned with such apparent windfall payments, however, for at least three reasons. First, the transpar-ency and improvement of data quality to make the COD Aid agreement work are important objectives in themselves. Second, paying recipients with successful public programs is much like giving budget support to a country that is generally a high performer—something many funders already do. Contrast this with the large number of projects that fully disburse their funds without achieving their goals, implying much more

> COD funds are no more likely to be subject to corruption than other aid

waste. Third, in most of the cases considered here (such as schools, health services, water), public policies generally contribute in some way to success, if only through supporting the basic administrative infrastructure necessary for service systems to function. So, in most of the cases we are discussing, it is very unlikely that progress could be achieved without some significant contribution from the public sector.

Difficulty measuring outcomes?

Identifying a relevant, credible, and feasible outcome measure is essential to the COD Aid approach, and there is no inherent reason that such measures cannot be designed. Meeting this challenge is a practical issue that, in many cases, can be resolved by convening experts and encouraging creative problem-solving. Our proposal in chapter 3 to measure progress toward universal primary education by testing students in their final year of primary school is the result of such a delibera-tive process. Ultimately, setting correct outcome measures can be assessed only in the context of a specific goal in a specific country, and in collaboration with local and international experts.

BOX 2.3
Fees or prizes?

Governments and philanthropies have used a range of methods to induce innovation. Cur-rent examples include grants for basic research, advance market commitments,[1] and payments for outcomes (such as the Global Alliance for Vaccines and Immunisation), as well as prizes.

Masters and Delbecq (2008) propose a proportional-reward prize system to encour-age higher agricultural productivity. The prize money would be fully disbursed at the end of the time period to participating farm-ers in proportion to the productivity gain each one achieves. That is, if all farmers in-creased their productivity by equal amounts, each would get an equal share of the prize money. If some farmers raised productivity dramatically more than their neighbors, they would get a proportionately larger share.

Incorporating this idea in a COD Aid agreement is possible if the agreement involves a number of countries competing

for the prize, and it is attractive for three reasons. First, it solves the problem facing funders over disbursement. With a prize, disbursement is guaranteed. Second, it complements the idea of a global compact that could be on offer to countries that wish to join (see box 2.2). Requirements for enter-ing the contest would focus on establishing baseline data and third-party verification. Third, countries would be rewarded in relation to the difficulty of the task. If all countries easily accelerate student achieve-ment, the average payment would be lower. But if the task is difficult, then only those countries that really put in the effort will be rewarded—and rewarded well.

A proportional-reward prize could be effective within countries too. For example, states could establish proportional-reward prizes for school districts or schools that choose to participate.

Note
1. Advance Market Commitment Working Group 2005.

No progress means no payment: political risks and external shocks
With the COD Aid approach, if the recipient makes no progress, the funder makes no payments. Funders take the risk that funds will not be disbursed, and recipients take the risk that any failures will be visibly and transparently revealed. This frequently expressed concern—viewing lack of disbursements as a risk—is somewhat strange in a broader perspective. If a contractor fails to construct a road, only the contractors are likely to be upset that the government refuses to pay them. If a recipient country fails to educate even one additional child, why would a funder want to pay it?

Of course, the failure to disburse foreign aid can create political problems for government aid agencies. Failure to disburse foreign aid can lead to cuts in subsequent aid requests and to charges of political failure to fulfill pledges.[13] This risk can be mitigated by establishing contingencies for the use of funds for other public purposes or by pooling the risk across a number of recipients. Another alternative is to structure the payment as a "prize" whose actual value would be determined by the number of children educated among a group of competing countries (box 2.3).

Failure to make progress and receive payments is also problematic for recipients. Even the best-intentioned recipients, with the best of plans, may not succeed due to factors beyond their control. External shocks to terms of trade, major crop failures, or serious financial crises can interfere with a country's progress on schooling in any one year. Fortunately, if the right policies and efforts are in place, there is likely to be catch-up progress in a subsequent year, with higher than expected payments compensating for the earlier lower payment. While it is tempting to protect countries from such delays, reducing the recipient's ultimate responsibility and discretion is the only way to mitigate this risk. Well intentioned efforts to limit the recipient's risk of failure weaken the COD Aid incentive. It changes COD Aid into an entitlement rather than a payment for achievement.

The one exception is to make explicit provision for factors beyond the recipient's control that jeopardize their efforts to measure and report outcomes, such as a natural disaster that interferes with testing. If factors beyond the recipients' control keep them from measuring progress in schools, provisions for extending deadlines may be required (chapter 4).

The official aid system, like other large systems, does not change rapidly. Enlightened staff of donor bureaucracies, well aware of the constraints to new products and modalities, have raised useful questions and concerns. In our view, most can be managed. Some are more like testable hypotheses (would governments respond to this kind of incentive?) and can be addressed only once COD Aid is tried. Our argument is not that COD Aid will solve all problems, but that its advantages make it well worth trying.

> If the recipient makes no progress, the funder makes no payments

COD Aid builds on other results-based aid programs

This chapter has discussed the essential features and basic steps of COD Aid. It has explored the many advantages and addressed concerns that this initiative raises. Before moving on to the detailed discussion in chapter 3, which applies COD Aid to education, we compare it with other results-based aid programs. Results-based programs implemented in recent years provide an experience base to learn from—and indeed have influenced our design of COD Aid. Drawing out comparisons with other results-based programs will allow us to further distinguish and introduce COD Aid, while making it clear how we have learned from and built on these earlier efforts.

Incremental payment

The Global Alliance for Vaccines and Immunisation (GAVI) is an alliance of public and private funders that provides funds and incentives for countries to expand and improve their immunization programs.[14] Countries present a plan for increasing childhood immunization rates. If approved, they receive an initial payment and become eligible for ex post rewards based on progress. GAVI's measure of progress is the number of children who have obtained all three antigens for diphtheria, tetanus, and pertussis (DTP-3) through vaccination. GAVI pays $20 per child, which was at one point estimated to be the cost of providing DTP-3 to a child in recipient countries.

The results element of GAVI is similar to the COD Aid proposal in that it provides an incremental payment for each unit of progress. GAVI also reduces the administrative burden on recipient countries by coordinating some funder support through a single mechanism and relying where possible on existing information systems.

GAVI differs from COD Aid, however, in that it provides a basic payment upfront and links only a part of funds to the outcome. In addition, the payment to recipient governments by GAVI is intended to help cover the costs of the immunization program, not to be used at the government's discretion in other sectors or programs. Another difference is that the GAVI arrangement relies on the country's reporting system to establish progress once that system has been vetted for reliability and accuracy, as opposed to COD Aid's independent audit. Although the country reporting systems are vetted ahead of time, problems have been discovered after the fact (see box 7.1 in chapter 7).

Output-based aid and other performance-based incentive programs

The results element of GAVI is similar to the COD Aid proposal

Output-based aid is a World Bank program sponsored by the U.K. Department for International Development, among others. Its payments to providers are linked to their delivery of specific physical outputs, such as paying private contractors for each water connection installed. In the health sector, funders have sponsored payments to NGOs based at least in part on such outputs as the number of prenatal visits.[15] Performance incentives have been paid to households as well. The best-known are conditional cash transfer programs under which, for example, mothers receive monthly cash payments conditional on their children attending school or making regular visits to health clinics.[16]

> **COD Aid aims to provide a clear incentive for top officials to focus on a key outcome**

These programs differ from COD Aid in two ways. First, they pay not for an outcome (such as improved health or learning) but for an output—the number of water connections or consultations at a clinic, or the fact that children attended school. Second, these programs operate at the micro level of providers or consumers. In contrast, COD Aid operates at the macro level. It aims to provide a clear incentive for top officials (heads of state, ministers of finance) to focus on a key outcome. Of course, top officials have the option of using COD Aid funds to create micro incentives for local providers or households. This enhances COD Aid's potential to make local providers and politicians accountable to their constituents.

Budget support

Budget support programs began in the 1990s as an effort to align aid with country priorities and systems, thus improving ownership. These programs also seek to reduce the administrative burden on recipients and to focus attention on shared objectives. To accomplish these aims, funders and recipients negotiate agreements that set objectives related to improving governance or public policies. The agreed objectives are specified in such inputs as minimum spending on poverty programs, such processes as streamlining public sector management, and such outputs as the number of schools built. Funds are then disbursed against periodic assessments of progress on this mix of inputs and processes, rather than disbursing funds against expenditures on specific activities. In practice, many budget support programs rely on other joint planning exercises such as Poverty Reduction Strategy Papers or Sector-Wide Approaches (SWAps).

A prominent evaluation of budget support programs was commissioned by funders. The report specifically endorsed the idea of linking payments to a broad range of indicators related to overall performance rather than linking them mechanically to specific outcomes. The report reasoned that conditions and indicators specified in budget support programs cannot focus on outcomes due to poor and infrequent data. The vagueness of indicators also gives different funders in any country the flexibility to apply their own judgments.[17]

Budget support programs provide a forum for funders and recipients to regularly discuss priorities and review performance in a number of dimensions. To the extent that performance is judged flexibly, it also makes disbursements more predictable. This is helpful to both funders and recipient governments for planning.

By its nature, however, budget support cannot be structured around a single clear outcome that is transparent to citizens and shared by the recipient government.

COD Aid complements budget support by adding far greater accountability

Indeed, recipient governments have sometimes seen the goals as onerous conditions. The multiple performance and progress measures of budget support and the different schedules of funder assistance make it less likely that recipient country citizens will understand what is occurring. Thus, recipient governments continue to be accountable primarily to their funders rather than their citizens. Budget support clearly cannot encourage and may even put at risk the responsiveness of government officials and politicians to their own citizens—on which the sustained growth and development that funders want to support depends.

COD Aid complements budget support by adding a far greater element of accountability. Like budget support, COD Aid payments are made to the government without restriction on the use of funds and are disbursed after assessing progress toward predefined goals and indicators. But unlike budget support, COD Aid:

- Is focused on one or very few measures, thus strengthening the incentive effect and reducing ambiguity on achievements.
- Pays against incremental measures of progress (such as numbers of students who graduate), thus making calculation of disbursements a less high-stakes, pass-fail process.
- Is verified by an independent third party, increasing the credibility of the commitment to pay only for the amount of progress achieved, no more and no less.
- Is likely to be more predictable because it depends more on factors within the recipients' control (progress) than on factors in the funder country (budget pressures or changing geopolitical concerns).

EC performance-linked budget support

The European Commission allocates budget support with a fixed and a variable tranche.[18] The variable tranche depends on whether the recipient has met mutually agreed targets for a range of public finance, health, and education indicators in the recipient government's Poverty Reduction Strategy Paper. To the extent that the variable tranche is linked to true outcome measures, it shares some aspects with COD Aid. The EC's budget support initiative differs from COD Aid, however, in that it contains a fairly large number of indicators, and most of the funds (more than 90 percent) are fixed, not linked to outcomes.

Time for a new approach

We believe it is time to try a new approach to aid—not to replace existing modalities but to experiment with a new one—with funders paying "cash" only on "delivery" of the agreed unit of progress. After extensive research, consultation, and review, we have devised an approach that focuses on shared goals and payment for outcomes, providing cash only on delivery of confirmed progress. The key features and basic steps outlined here, the advantages such a system could generate, the valid concerns that can be answered, and the improvements on other recent limited reforms encourage us to see COD Aid as the initiative now needed in foreign aid.

COD Aid will not be a panacea, but it will directly address many of the commitments in the 2005 Paris Declaration, against which little progress has been made thus far. Among other characteristics, COD Aid:

- Generates accountability for results by firmly linking payments to outcomes that represent measures of progress toward a shared goal.
- Involves full ownership by recipient governments who have complete flexibility to choose how to accomplish the goal, allowing for local self-discovery and institutional development;
- Improves learning about what works because the contract creates incentives for measuring outcomes rather than inputs, generating data on progress in addition to expenditures.
- Guarantees harmonization and alignment because it involves a single agreement with each country no matter how many funders are involved.
- Makes predictability of funding a function of recipient country planning and performance and less a function of funder politics and budgets.

Our COD Aid proposal cannot eliminate the political pressures and conflicts that undermine aid effectiveness. It does, however, create structures that confine those pressures to the initial contract negotiation phase. It also permits funders and recipients to focus on their joint objectives rather than their divergent interests. Once a funder and recipient have agreed to the terms of the COD Aid contract, it becomes difficult to divert attention from the shared goal.

Moving to COD Aid will not be simple. Both recipients and funders will have to relinquish a comfortable way of doing business for something untried. But if funders and recipients look openly at the tradeoffs, we believe they will see the value in trying this approach. The essential tradeoffs for each party can be characterized as follows:

- In return for accepting the public contract, funders will not be able to control design or determine inputs, and any engagement in implementation will depend on whether the recipient requests it. They will, however, be able to respond to demands for accountability in their own countries because of the simplicity and transparency of linking payments to progress. They will also benefit by sending foreign aid only to countries that have genuinely improved their development outcomes.

  Both recipients and funders will have to relinquish a comfortable way of doing business

- In return for accepting the public contract, recipients will receive COD Aid payments only if they achieve agreed outcomes. In return, however, they will have complete discretion and responsibility for their domestic programs, will choose whether and from whom to seek technical assistance, and will redirect their information gathering efforts away from input monitoring reports and toward outcome measurement and analysis.

It would be presumptuous to claim that this proposal is ensured of success or even that it will be more successful than other aid modalities. But our view is that COD Aid addresses the difficult problems of accountability in foreign aid more fully than existing modalities. In this sense, it represents an approach that is well worth trying, adapting, and assessing.

The next step in fully exploring COD Aid is to consider it in a particular context. The success of a COD Aid agreement will hinge on a number of important details: the likelihood of reaching agreement on shared goals, the exact character of the outcome measure to avoid undesirable side effects, the right fee schedule to ensure an adequate incentive, an effective and credible audit process to minimize incentives for the recipient country to manipulate data, contingencies to deal with unforeseen setbacks, provisions to ensure that the COD Aid is additional to existing funding, and mechanisms to make the funder's commitment credible. Chapter 3 is an opportunity to engage COD Aid at this level of detail, examining how COD Aid might be applied in education to achieve the goal of reaching universal primary completion in developing countries.

Notes

1. This would not be unprecedented. The World Bank has arrangements with some member governments under which those governments buy technical advisory services from the Bank, just as they might from a private consultancy.
2. EQUIP2 n.d.-a, n.d.-b; Rajani 2005.
3. High Level Forum on Aid Effectiveness 2005, Development Assistance Committee 2008b.
4. In fact, sometimes the inputs chosen seem to be driven more by donor trends than anything else (Rodrik 2007).
5. For the limitations of current approaches to participation, see Birdsall (2008) and World Bank (2004).
6. See Eichler and Levine (2009) for case studies of such performance payments to a range of health care providers.
7. Harding 2009.
8. Birdsall (2007) lists 20 such countries.
9. For a definition of fragile states, see OECD (2006).
10. See Barder and Birdsall (2006).
11. A good example is the International Finance Facility for Immunizations, initially backed by the U.K. government and the Bill and Melinda Gates Foundation; see IFFIm (2008).
12. DFID and others 2004; World Bank n.d.; PEFA 2005.

13. The U.S. Millennium Challenge Account has struggled with this political challenge. Countries must compete for its funds and then design and implement its compacts. While this has advantages over other forms of aid, it can create a greater lag from commitment to disbursement; see Herrling and Rose (2007).

14. Chee and others 2004; Hsi and Fields 2004.

15. Eichler and Levine 2009.

16. On conditional cash transfers, see Morley and Coady (2003) and Eichler and Levine (2009), among others.

17. The International Development Department and Associates (2006) report was conducted as part of the Joint Evaluation of General Budget Support commissioned by a consortium of funding agencies and seven recipient governments under the auspices of the Development Assistance Committee Network on Development Evaluation. The report specifically endorsed the idea of linking payments to a broad range of indicators related to overall performance rather than linking them mechanically to specific outcomes. The report reasoned that conditions and indicators specified in budget support programs cannot focus on outcomes due to poor and infrequent data. For funders, the vagueness of indicators allows each the flexibility to apply its own judgment (see, in particular, pages 36, 68–69, and 98–99). The report noted that different funder decisions are inconsistent: they make their own decisions about disbursements based on common data but apply different rules and judgments.

18. European Commission 2005.

Applications of
Cash on Delivery Aid

Part II

Applying COD Aid to primary education: a contract between partners

Cash on Delivery Aid (COD Aid) could be applied in many sectors and in a variety of financial relationships. But is it practical? In this chapter we explain how foreign aid agencies could use COD Aid to collaborate with developing countries in reaching universal primary schooling. Applying COD Aid to this specific example illustrates the kinds of problems to be addressed and demonstrates that most of them are manageable. The challenges seem no greater than those that arise with traditional aid modalities. (In chapter 4 we turn to practical issues of funding and implementation.)

Essential elements of a COD Aid agreement for primary education

As chapter 2 discussed, COD Aid has five key features: payment for outcomes, hands-off funders and responsible recipients, independent verification, transparency through public dissemination, and complementarity with existing aid programs. In practical terms, this requires that a COD Aid contract include four essential elements:

- A shared and clearly defined goal.
- A unit for measuring progress.
- Payment per unit of progress.
- A system for measuring and verifying progress.

The first essential element is a goal that is shared by both funder and recipient and is clearly defined. If the goal is not genuinely shared, or is ancillary to other hidden objectives (such as tied aid, geopolitical allegiance of the funder, or other domestic priorities of the recipient), there is no point in embarking on a COD Aid agreement. Especially with full recipient discretion and responsibility, little progress will be made unless the goal merits real commitment from both parties. The implementation of the agreement

A COD Aid
contract includes
a system for
measuring and
verifying progress

also requires that the goal be sufficiently specified to permit accurate measurement and verification.

The second element of a COD Aid contract is a unit for measuring progress toward the shared goal. The unit of measurement should be relevant, precise, and capable of capturing continuous or incremental progress.

A definite statement of the amount to be paid for each unit of progress is the third essential element. That amount is not pegged to the cost of progress—it should be in proportion to the amount needed to attract the attention, energy, and commitment of high-level policy actors.

The final element of any COD Aid contract is a system for measuring and verifying progress. That system includes the means for a recipient to collect data on progress, the data the recipient collects, and the provision for third-party verification of data.

This chapter describes a hypothetical COD Aid agreement in the education sector. In this example, the four essential elements are embodied as follows:

- The shared goal is to ensure that every child completes primary education of good quality.
- The unit of progress is an "assessed completer," a student who is enrolled in the last year of primary school and who takes an approved standardized test.
- The funder agrees to pay $20 for each student who takes a standardized test in the last year of primary school up to the total enrollment in the base year and $200 for each assessed completer in excess of that number.
- The recipient commits to disseminating its information on student enrollments, assessed completers and test scores (at some agreed level of disaggregation). The funder commits to contracting a third party to verify the accuracy of the recipient's reports.

Box 3.1 provides a summary of the proposed contract. The rest of the chapter discusses the rationale behind the choices in preparing this contract. The appendix contains term sheets that could be used to negotiate such a contract.

Shared goal: universal primary completion

A good example of a shared goal in a COD Aid contract is to ensure that every child completes primary education of good quality. Universal primary education is an appropriate goal for such an agreement because it has already been endorsed by many countries, both in international agreements and in domestic policies. In September 2000, 189 countries signed the UN Millennium Declaration, which calls for universalizing primary school. Universal primary education is one of the eight Millennium Development Goals subsequently agreed.[1] Most countries have constitutional provisions or at least national legislation guaranteeing their population's access to primary schooling.

BOX 3.1
Outline for a COD Aid contract to pay for assessed completers

1. The funder commits to pay the recipient government $20 per assessed completer up to the total number of children enrolled in the last year of primary school in the base year and $200 per assessed completer beyond that number.
2. The contract is for five years, extendable in five-year increments.
3. Only students enrolled in the last year of primary schooling are eligible to be counted as assessed completers for the COD Aid agreement.
4. The funder will pay only once for each student, regardless of how many times he or she may repeat or retake the test.
5. The funder will contract an agent from a preapproved list of organizations to verify the government's report on the number of assessed completers and their scores.
6. The agent will retest a randomly selected sample of schools and disseminate the findings publicly.
7. If the retest findings show the official reports are accurate within a 5 percent margin, the COD payment will be calculated as described in item 1. Otherwise, the COD payment will be reduced to reflect the agent's estimate along with a penalty.
8. The participating funder commits to ensuring that the COD payments are treated as additional to other assistance to the country.
9. At the inception of the contract, the funder will place a guarantee in escrow equivalent to the amount that would be disbursed over the subsequent two years if the country were able to test 90 percent of the base year enrollment in the last year of primary school. The funder will replenish the escrow account annually so that, in any given year, the account holds enough funds for the subsequent two years based on mutually agreed projections.
10. Funders will designate an account to which countries may charge up to 90 percent of the direct costs of developing a robust information system on student completion and of developing and rolling out the standardized competency test.
11. The standardized competency test will be designed to allow accurate tracking of learning outcomes from year to year in order to assess whether schooling quality is improving and to assist management and education policy decisions.
12. The recipient commits to publicly report student completion figures and average test scores, with levels of disaggregation appropriate to the accuracy and reliability of the test, to be agreed as a part of the contract.
13. The recipient commits to allow and facilitate research into education policy, the development of institutions, and the effects of the contract, and to make complete individual-level education data and public finance data available to researchers for this purpose, with appropriate measures taken to protect the privacy of all individuals.
14. The funders and recipient agree that, in the event of a dispute, they will follow procedures to select and abide by the decisions of an international arbitration panel.

Despite the shared commitment to reaching the Millennium Development Goal of universal primary completion by 2015, many countries are unlikely to reach it (figure 3.1). COD Aid is a way to reinvigorate efforts and accelerate progress in these

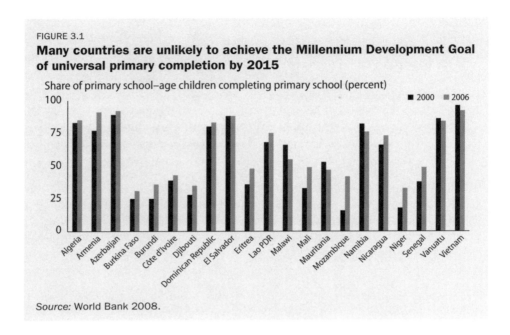

FIGURE 3.1

Many countries are unlikely to achieve the Millennium Development Goal of universal primary completion by 2015

Share of primary school–age children completing primary school (percent)

Source: World Bank 2008.

countries; one reviewer even described the COD Aid proposal as "Millennium Development Goals with teeth."

Measure of progress: assessed completers

The next element is to identify an indicator that would measure progress toward the shared goal. In this example, we propose that progress be measured by the number of assessed completers—that is, the number of students enrolled in the last year of primary school who complete a standardized test.[2] This measure has several advantages:

- It is easily defined.
- It is closely related to the goal of universal primary education.
- It draws attention to the content and quality of schooling.
- It is relatively easy to audit.
- It encourages the development of management information and testing systems.

Number of assessed completers is easily defined

Why count the number of students taking a test to measure increases in completion when school records could be used instead? First, the definition of completing primary school is problematic. Many countries lack a clear definition of what is required to complete the cycle in terms of minimum attendance, learning standards, or performance on any formal system of assessment for progressing through the school system and graduating. As a result, most international data on the number of children who complete primary school are little more than the difference between the number of students who enroll in the last year of primary school minus the number who are held back to repeat that year.[3] Countries that lack a clear definition of primary school completion would need to negotiate such a standard with the funder, and verification would require a detailed audit to assess whether the standard has been met. Such an undertaking would be expensive, requiring an audit of attendance records among other things. By contrast, the number of students taking a test is clearly defined and fairly simple to measure.

Number of assessed completers is related to the goal of universal primary education

An assessed completer is not exactly equivalent to ensuring that every child completes a good quality primary education, for a variety of reasons. Students may be absent for a large number of school days or be poorly taught. Even so, the test scores will give some indication of the share and number of students who have mastered the educational content that is expected of students who complete primary school.

Number of assessed completers draws attention to the content and quality of schooling

If no test were administered, recipients might be tempted to expand enrollment at the expense of school quality. By paying for the number of last-year students who take a test, the proposed COD Aid contract ensures that the quality of schooling is not ignored. The requirement that these test scores be published—disaggregated to a level that is appropriate and feasible—draws attention to the content of schooling and the performance of schools. This is likely to facilitate public debate about the quality and equity of the education system. Public dissemination also encourages the government to respond more to concerns of civil society than to concerns of funders. Furthermore, the education community will be able to use the published test scores in interpreting results and improving the assessment system. Although our proposed indicator does not make payment contingent on achieving any individual or aggregate test scores, public dissemination of the results is required and should help make government and school systems more accountable for progress on quality as well as quantity of schooling. Over time, this may be one of the most valuable aspects of the agreement.

> **Public dissemination of results should make government and school systems more accountable for progress**

Number of assessed completers is relatively easy to audit

Verifying the number of assessed completers is much easier than verifying the number of students who complete primary school. Auditors need only check the number of students who took a test on a particular day, rather than verify that students have completed some minimum attendance over a long period. The tasks, scale, and duration of the audit can be precisely defined, and the opportunities for manipulating and cheating

A COD Aid
contract
encourages
countries to
improve their
administrative
information

are reasonably limited. In addition, the audit can take place a week or two after the initial test, providing timely feedback on the accuracy of the indicator that will trigger payments (see further details below under reporting and verification).

Number of assessed completers encourages the development of management information and testing systems

A COD Aid contract that pays for assessed completers encourages countries to administer externally validated tests that give useful feedback to national policymakers, state governments, school districts, schools, teachers, students, and parents. It encourages countries to improve their administrative information so they can better track who is and is not in school, fostering the development of domestic capacity to assess students and analyze student performance. The benefits of testing and publishing data also mean that even if the COD Aid agreement results in few additional students completing school, the aid has still accomplished something of substantial value: improving the evidence base for effective policymaking.

A standardized test of learning provides policymakers and parents with useful and comparable information.[4] The COD Aid contract to pay for assessed completers could be associated with any particular test that is mutually agreeable to the funder and the recipient. But to reflect the shared goal of reaching universal primary school completion, the test should relate to the learning expected at that level. The most appropriate and feasible test for such a purpose would probably be a standardized test of competencies or skills (such as basic reading, writing, and mathematics) commonly acquired on completing primary school. The test should also be able to discern changes in learning from cohort to cohort over time.

To be useful for education policy, such standards-based assessments do not need to be comparable across countries. But they do need to be stable over time in a number of ways. They should test the same age cohorts and measure the same content or competencies. Measurement instruments should be at the same levels of difficulty and reliability. Empirical equating—ensuring that the tests are measuring the same constructs, have the same reliability, and are population invariant—should be conducted to confirm the equivalence of the test content and results over time.[5]

Tests based on representative samples must use the same sampling procedure from year to year. Those based on a full student census need to collect enough information to control for the changing composition of students from year to year. And the country must have the capacity to scientifically design, administer, score, and analyze the test or must be willing to outsource or purchase services that it cannot itself provide.

Few developing countries fulfill all these criteria with current national assessments. At most, 20 low- and middle-income countries conduct annual national learning assessments. The analysis needed to judge the reliability of the tests is not generally completed, and few tests have been calibrated through empirical equating. Many low- and middle-income countries are making substantial progress toward routine application and use of national learning assessments, but they might find it challenging to design and implement such a test in the short run. They could use or adapt an existing international or regional test that meets the same standards while beginning the process of developing their own national test to meet these standards, or could choose to rely on existing international and regional tests for the long run.[6]

> **Deciding exactly which dimensions to measure is a valuable part of national policy debates**

To avoid intrusiveness with assistance in test development, the recipient should choose whether and which firm or agency to contract with for technical support. The firm or agency could be selected from a number of organizations with appropriate expertise, including testing firms, international agencies such as the United Nations Educational, Scientific, and Cultural Organization, and organizations that have implemented international and regional learning assessments in recent years.[7] This is the one activity for which we recommend that the funder provide financial resources upfront, but the choice of whether and with whom to seek assistance remains the recipient's responsibility (box 3.2).

Testing must measure what society wants children to learn

Testing students serves many purposes.[8] Sometimes it is meant to select students for placement in subsequent levels of instruction or jobs; sometimes it is used to assess student performance as feedback for the student, parents, and teacher. At other times it is aimed at assessing the quality of the schooling system itself. All testing can be controversial. Education is a complex and multifaceted process, and no test can possibly measure all its various dimensions. Even so, properly executed tests can measure some aspects of education.

The process of deciding exactly which dimensions to measure is itself a valuable part of national policy debates. Introducing national tests, even when rewards and penalties are not associated with results, is likely to encourage teachers and schools to teach material and skills that are tested—that is, to teach to the test. In itself this is not a bad thing so long as the test is valid and reliable and measures the key outcomes that a society expects from its children's education. This practice becomes a serious problem only when the test becomes the sole focus of education to the exclusion of other less easily measured aspects of schooling.

But be careful how you use tests due to weak validity, high stakes, and cheating

Once a test is required, it is tempting to condition the payment on student test performance. But our consultations with experts and review of previous experiences

BOX 3.2
Paying upfront costs for test development and implementation

The COD Aid contract is designed to channel resources toward governments as they make progress on outcomes on which they and funders have already agreed to focus effort. This is why the COD Aid contract does not include advance funding for investments to expand and improve education. Funds from both foreign aid and domestic revenues should already be available for improving and expanding education; the additional COD Aid funds would flow as the government implements these programs and improves them. But the COD Aid contract does require one additional task for funds to flow: accurate reporting on outcomes.

Developing and implementing a national competency test, or upgrading an existing test to meet the standards described here, require upfront expenditure, as do assigning unique identifiers to students and upgrading existing education management information systems to enable accurate reporting of outcomes. The amount required will depend on the country and the systems already in place, but could range from a few hundred thousand dollars to a few million dollars.

Funders routinely provide aid to develop such systems because of the benefits for policymaking. Much of this aid is delivered in traditional input-driven ways, including packages of technical assistance to build local capacity to collect and manage the information. Such aid is often tied to providers of services and expertise from funding countries or at least to particular approaches. For reasons discussed earlier, much of this aid has failed. For example, much funding and expertise are invested without successfully equating a test or getting statistics to agree. But if efforts to develop stronger information systems were linked to the prospect of major flexible funding that would be available once a country qualified for cash payments, this might muster the focus and political will that could make the difference. Different parts of the bureaucracy might be pressured to get together and find out why their statistics disagree or wait to release test scores until they have been properly standardized.

We propose that funders incorporate a mechanism to help cover the direct upfront costs required to improve administrative reporting and information management enough to implement the COD Aid contract. Funders would agree to cover a certain percentage of eligible costs (say, 90 percent) with a predetermined ceiling and without requiring preapproval. The recipient could contract directly with providers of such services as test development and then send the bill to the funder.

have convinced us that this temptation has to be resisted. As discussed below, questions about test score validity and reliability will take time to resolve, and conditioning payments on scores that later prove to have been faulty could undermine the credibility of the entire project of testing. Meanwhile, staking large financial rewards on test performance encourages manipulation of results—by the recipient, schools, or even pupils. Such cheating increases the cost of auditing, reduces the utility of test scores for policymaking, and undermines efforts to introduce worthwhile student assessments. For these reasons, we propose that the payment be based on the number of children who take the exam and not on their test scores.

How many assessed completers are additional?

Which assessed completers would be paid for: all assessed completers or only those who would not have completed primary schooling without the COD Aid agreement? The ideal measure would be the difference between the actual number of assessed completers and a baseline calculated as a projection of how many students would have completed primary school without the COD Aid agreement. But any effort to project such a baseline would require extensive assumptions and the complications this entails would undermine the transparency of the agreement.

After reviewing this dilemma, we came to the conclusion that the baseline should be as simple as possible to facilitate transparency and reduce the risks of projecting a counterfactual future. Our proposal, therefore, is to calculate the number of additional assessed completers as the difference between the actual number of assessed completers and a baseline comprising the number of students who completed primary school in the first year of the program (base-year enrollment). If the agreement is extended beyond five years, as planned, then the baseline would be adjusted to the number of assessed completers five years earlier (the baseline would become completion with a five-year lag).

Adjusting the baseline is important for at least two reasons. First, it avoids a sharp drop in payments when universal completion is reached. Second, it strengthens the incentive to make additional effort to reach universal completion since every five years the payments associated with earlier achievements are removed.

The size of the payment

The COD Aid agreement has to establish how much the country will receive for each unit of progress. One approach is to calculate the cost of educating each student and use that as the basis for setting the payment. But the cost of educating students varies substantially across countries, across regions within countries, and across socioeconomic groups. Using the average cost could be seen as harmful to subpopulations or regions where the costs of schooling are higher than average. If, however, the fixed payment varied across countries, regions, or socioeconomic groups, it would seem to imply that the value placed on educating a child in one place is higher than for educating a child in another place. Above all, the idea of linking the payment to costs deflects attention from the real purpose of the payment: to be an incentive for the recipient to make progress toward what has already been agreed is a priority. Ultimately, countries are themselves committed to educating all their children and expect to do so in a financially sustainable fashion in the future. Thus, the COD Aid payment is not really aimed at covering the cost of schooling. It is aimed at relaxing constraints that hold back progress.

> The COD Aid payment is aimed at relaxing constraints that hold back progress

**$200 per
assessed
completer would
get the attention
of policymakers
and engage them
in improving
efficiency**

A payment of $200 per student could be sufficient incentive

After consulting with a wide range of people from developing country governments, bilateral aid agencies, multilateral institutions, foundations, and research centers, we came to the conclusion that $200 per assessed completer would be appropriate. This amount is large enough so that the expected funds would be significant relative to the government's education budget and existing foreign aid flows. It would get the attention of policymakers and engage them in improving efficiency. And it would provide enough resources to expand existing programs (school construction, teacher training, additional school bus routes) or create new ones (school meals, paved rural roads).

Although the payment could be negotiated in several ways, a very promising approach would be for multiple interested funders and recipients to agree on a single global price, perhaps in the context of a big push to accelerate progress toward the education Millennium Development Goal. This would uphold the notion of equality among beneficiaries and simultaneously provide lower income countries with more resources since their domestic costs are lower (see box 2.1).

A practical consideration: initial payments for implementing testing

For most countries, implementing a new test will be financially challenging. For practical reasons, then, it makes sense for funders to compensate the recipient for the cost of testing in the first few years. Based on international learning assessments, these costs could range between $5 and $25 per student.[9] We recommend that the COD Aid agreement in a typical low-income country include paying $20 for testing of each assessed completer up to the number of students enrolled in the last year of primary school when the agreement is signed. This payment would be phased out over five years. The number of assessed completers in excess of the base year enrollment would, of course, be compensated at the higher rate of $200 per assessed completer (box 3.3).

Total sums must be substantial enough to provide an incentive

The sums provided for progress must be substantial enough to provide an incentive for the recipient country. COD Aid payments can be put in the context of overall education budgets and foreign aid with an example from a low-income developing country in Sub-Saharan Africa. It has a population of about 35 million and a net enrollment in the last year of primary school of 64 percent of the children in the same age cohort. A payment of $200 per additional assessed completer in this case would imply annual transfers of between $10 million and $30 million if the recipient country reached 100 percent completion (box 3.4 and table 3.1). After this, the payments would gradually decline (see box 3.3 for details on the payment formula). This sum would still represent a fairly small share of total education spending in the country and only about 10–20

BOX 3.3
Formula for calculating the payment

The key elements of the payment formula in the text are:

1. Payments of $200 are made for each additional assessed completer.
2. The number of additional assessed completers is calculated as the difference between the actual number of assessed completers and the baseline.
3. The baseline is equal to base year enrollment (the number of assessed completers in the program's first year) during the program's first five years. The baseline is adjusted thereafter to be the number of assessed completers five years earlier.
4. Payments to implement testing are made during the first five years at the rate of $20 for each assessed completer and are phased out over this period.

To express this formally, during the first five years, the formula for payment for the additional assessed completers in year t would be:

$$\$200 * (AC_t - AC_b), \text{ when } AC_t > AC_b$$

where AC_t is the number of assessed completers in year t and AC_b is the number of assessed completers in the first year of the contract.

Assuming that, after five years, the country is testing more students than five years earlier ($AC_t > AC_{t-5}$), the formula for payments would then change to:

$$\$200 * (AC_t - AC_{t-5})$$

The payment for implementing testing can be expressed formally as:

$$P * AC_t$$

where AC_t is the number of assessed completers in year t, as before, and P is a payment that declines over five years: $20 per assessed completer for years 1 and 2, $15 for year 3, $10 for year 4, and $5 for year 5.

An illustration of the amounts of money involved for a typical developing country is shown in figure 1 in box 3.4 and in table 3.1.

percent of foreign aid to education (in African countries with per capita incomes below $5,000, primary education spending ranges from $20 to $800 per student).

In our view, the small amounts are likely to provide substantial incentives for at least two reasons. First, they would be attractive because they can be used flexibly, unlike the current largely committed spending for teacher salaries and other costs. Second, the public nature and transparency of the COD Aid contract means that all funds create reputational risks (and opportunities) for political leaders. In any event, the suggested size of the payment is meant to provide a starting point for funder-recipient negotiations; the actual payment specified in the contract would be the outcome of those negotiations.

Reporting and verification

Transparent reporting and verification are essential to the COD Aid agreement
Reporting and verification through audits ensure mutual accountability, provide incentives to improve education data management systems and enable social audits (box 3.5).[10] Constituents of both funders and recipients will find COD Aid agreements

BOX 3.4
Illustration of COD Aid payments to a developing country

To illustrate the financial implications of a hypothetical COD Aid contract, we applied the payment formula (see box 3.3) to data characteristic of a low-income Sub-Saharan country with a population of about 35 million. About 330,000 graduate each year from primary school, or almost two-thirds of the 517,000 children in the same age cohort.

The assumption that completion will increase at a rate between 2 and 3 percent higher than the historical average yields an annual COD Aid payment of $4 million in the agreement's second year (predominantly covering the cost of testing for the baseline enrollment), rising to $30 million at its peak after 13 years and declining to zero after 22 years, when all students in the slowly increasing age cohort are completing primary school (see figures 1 and 2). For comparison, funders provided the country with about $30 million for basic education and $70 million for the entire education sector in 2005.

Source: Table 3.1.

FIGURE 1
Progression of COD Aid payments over 22 years

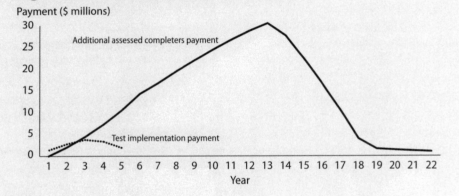

FIGURE 2
Number of enrolled students in final year of primary school

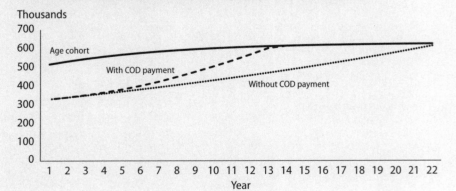

TABLE 3.1
Illustration of COD Aid payments to a developing country (thousands)

Year	Age cohort	Predicted final year enrollment Without COD Aid	Predicted final year enrollment With COD Aid	Baseline minus five years	Assessed completers[a]	Additional assessed completers[b]	Additional assessed completers payment ($)	Test implementation payment ($)	Total payment ($)
0	327.0								
1	517.2	331.0	331.0	331.0	66.2			1,324	1,324
2	532.7	340.9	340.9	331.0	136.4	9.9	1,986	2,727	4,713
3	546.3	351.2	352.9	331.0	247.0	21.9	4,373	3,705	8,078
4	558.1	361.7	367.0	331.0	330.3	36.0	7,195	3,303	10,498
5	568.4	372.5	383.5	331.0	383.5	52.5	10,498	1,917	12,416
6	577.3	383.7	402.7	340.9	402.7	71.7	14,333		14,333
7	585.0	395.2	424.8	352.9	424.8	83.9	16,776		16,776
8	591.6	407.1	450.3	367.0	450.3	97.4	19,488		19,488
9	597.3	419.3	477.3	383.5	477.3	110.3	22,068		22,068
10	602.2	431.9	506.0	402.7	506.0	122.5	24,493		24,493
11	606.4	444.8	536.3	424.8	536.3	133.7	26,730		26,730
12	610.0	458.2	568.5	450.3	568.5	143.7	28,736		28,736
13	613.0	471.9	602.6	477.3	602.6	152.3	30,461		30,461
14	615.6	486.1	615.6	506.0	615.6	138.3	27,666		27,666
15	617.9	500.7	617.9	536.3	617.9	111.9	22,384		22,384
16	619.8	515.7	619.8	568.5	619.8	83.5	16,694		16,694
17	621.4	531.2	621.4	602.6	621.4	52.9	10,583		10,583
18	622.8	547.1	622.8	615.6	622.8	20.2	4,038		4,038
19	624.0	563.5	624.0	617.9	624.0	8.3	1,665		1,665
20	625.0	580.4	625.0	619.8	625.0	7.1	1,419		1,419
21	625.8	597.8	625.8	621.4	625.8	6.0	1,209		1,209
22	626.6	615.8	626.6	621.4	626.6	5.2	1,030		1,030

a. Assumes that the test will be phased in gradually over five years, testing 20 percent, 50 percent, 70 percent, 90 percent, and 100 percent of the enrolled students each successive year and 100 percent thereafter. For the first five years, the baseline equals the enrollment from year one; from year six on, the baseline equals the enrollment from five years prior.
b. The number of assessed completers minus the baseline. Final year enrollment is used for years one through four, before testing covers all students.
Source: Authors' calculations using data from a Sub-Saharan African country with 64 percent primary completion rate in 2005.

BOX 3.5
What role can social audits play?

COD Aid emphasizes that funds should be disbursed against a specific measurable outcome. The main risk is that the incentive would encourage the recipient to make decisions that achieve the measurable outcome at the expense of other important goals. In education, the primary concern is that basing payments on the number of students could privilege quantity over quality.

Rather than weakening the incentive of a single clearly measurable outcome, our judgment is that additional instruments should be found to mitigate this risk. The most promising avenue is to rely on and strengthen a country's mechanisms for ensuring public accountability. For example, we propose that a COD Aid program for education pay for the number of students who take a test and simultaneously require that test scores be publicly disseminated. This is a necessary, though not sufficient, condition for civil society to pressure government to maintain and improve the quality of education.

This mechanism is often referred to as a social audit—information about public services is periodically collected, processed, and disseminated to strengthen public accountability and improve services. This is an ongoing process in any democratic country (publishing government budgets, reporting to legislatures on public services). But initiatives to explicitly introduce social audits in developing countries have met with varying success.

- In Bangalore, India, the Public Affairs Centre developed a citizen report card to measure citizen satisfaction with public services. Publicly disclosing and debating the citizen report cards led several public agencies to improve their services.[1]
- Community-based monitoring of health care services in Uganda had a demonstrable effect on improving health outcomes.[2]
- A Mexican nongovernmental organization established to review public budget information discovered that 30 million pesos earmarked for women's health programs had been diverted to purposes contrary to the government's HIV/AIDS prevention policies. The funds were later returned to their intended use.[3]
- A South African nongovernmental organization used budget data to document disparities and declines in child support grants. Subsequent public pressure led the government to increase and reapportion funding.[4]

Social audits are not foolproof, and other experiences demonstrate conditions under which they may fail to generate government responses (Banerjee, Banerji, and others 2008). But for trying a new aid modality such as COD Aid, experience shows that including mechanisms to facilitate social audits is a promising avenue.

Notes
1. Ravindra 2004.
2. Björkman and Svensson 2007.
3. Ramkumar 2008 [add to references].
4. de Renzio and Krafchik 2007.

much more credible if they have access to easily understood and reliable information. COD Aid contracts should therefore clearly specify the reporting and verification that must be fulfilled before payment is made.

Public reports of progress will then be used by the funder for calculating payments, and by a broader audience of policymakers, legislators, media, civil society, and parent groups. Through reports on test taking and test scores, they will begin to understand, interpret, and engage public policymakers, holding them accountable for the education system's performance in improving access, quality, and equity. Public disclosure of the verification reports would also allow civil society organizations and the public to assess the government's integrity and to pressure schools or administrators who fail to report or who manipulate information.

The reporting and verification also provide incentives to improve education data. In most developing countries, education system information is unreliable. For example, despite considerable investment in South Africa's Education Management Information System, the country still has no agreement on the actual number of schools in the country, let alone the number of students completing primary school. In such circumstances, the fact that the COD Aid agreement pays against officially reported information subject to an audit is likely to stimulate better recordkeeping.

The COD Aid contract requires four levels of disclosure.

The recipient would be expected to publicly disclose information at four levels:

- *Information on the test design and administration according to current professional standards.* This would allow technical experts to debate and judge the validity and reliability of the test and to offer comments to improve the national learning assessment.

- *The number of assessed completers and average test scores at a level of disaggregation specified in the contract (state, municipal, district, or school).* The disaggregation should be to the smallest level possible, given the test's validity, reliability, and precision. Because the national learning assessment will probably improve over time, the funder and recipient might agree to a fairly broad aggregation that becomes more refined.

- *The raw data to researchers, taking appropriate measures to protect the privacy of individuals who took the tests.* Providing open access to raw data increases the chances that worthwhile analysis will emerge, that suggestions for improvement will arise, and that errors will be detected. (We discuss country research on COD Aid in chapter 5.)

- *The results of the audit, as discussed below.*

The role of an audit

The independent audit of the number of assessed completers should be the subject of a separate contract between funders and a third-party auditor (see the model contract in the appendix). The independence of the

> **Paying against officially reported information subject to an audit is likely to stimulate better recordkeeping**

audit, contracted by the funder, is a critical part of the agreement.[11] The audit provides all parties with greater confidence in the outcome measures and assists the country in identifying any problems with its information system so that improvements can be made. To detect problems, the audit requires that each student have a unique identifying number, that the auditor apply a retest in a random sample of schools, and that consequences for discovered discrepancies are clearly specified.

Unique identification is required for an accurate audit. The first requirement for an accurate audit is to track who is and is not eligible to take the test. At a minimum, this requires that each assessed completer be assigned a unique identification number. Preferably, the official testing system would use a national identification number to identify each student. Numbers for national identification cards would serve such a purpose without requiring a substantial investment. With a unique identifier, the audit can detect double counting, repeated test taking, and other problems that could lead to inflated reports. If a country introduced identification numbers for students as a part of the COD Aid agreement, this would also benefit data management. For example, in some developing countries, students whose families migrate from one part of the country to another may be registered as dropouts in their original schools even though they have enrolled elsewhere, leading to inaccuracies that make management of the education system more challenging. A national identification number system would help address this.

Retesting a random sample of schools. To verify the number of assessed completers, the audit would include not only cross-checks of student identification numbers, but also a retest in a random sample of schools within a fairly short period of time after the official test (such as one or two weeks).[12] The retest would require assembling a team that can visit a number of schools throughout the country and administer a retest for all eligible children in those schools. In addition, the team would check identification numbers against electronic databases and inspect enrollment records. This retest could detect whether tests were being applied properly and reduce cheating by comparing test scores. It could also identify ineligible test takers and problems with enrollment records.

> **The audit provides all parties with greater confidence in the outcome measures**

To maximize attendance for the retest, the date of the retest would be publicized, but no one would know beforehand which schools were to be retested. Provisions for test security would ensure that test records are not tampered with after the retest.

Although the actual cost and scale of the audit would vary across countries, data from current international tests suggest that estimates with sufficient precision can be derived from retesting a sample of about 180 schools, involving about 9,000 students (box 3.6). The official reports would be accepted as accurate if the reported test scores

BOX 3.6
Cost and resources required for the audit

The sample size necessary to estimate average test scores for each school with a confidence interval of 5 percent depends on average test scores and their variance. Experience with international tests suggests these numbers might be 250 for average test scores with a standard deviation of 100. Creating a one-sided 95 percent confidence interval for the average school results with a width of 12.5 (5 percent of 250) would then require a sample size of about 180 schools. Assuming an average of 50 students per school would imply retesting about 9,000 students, which is close to the size of sample-based testing used by the Programme for International Student Assessment.

Field work would require about two person-days per school to administer the test and inspect school or district enrollment records. Further analysis would be required to derive useful results and report them in an understandable form. The cost of such an audit would be about $250,000 in addition to the basic cost of developing and applying the official test.

Source: Crouch and Mitchell 2008.

are less than a threshold calculated as a one-sided confidence interval derived from the retest sample.

The total cost could be as low as $250,000 if the audit can rely on an existing system of unique identification numbers (such as a national identity card system), reasonable data on how many primary schools the country has and where they are located, and access to an existing test that meets the necessary standards. Should it be necessary to create an identification number, conduct a census of primary schools, or develop a test without any prior groundwork, the costs would be correspondingly higher. Even with these additional costs, however, the total expenditure would be modest relative to the amount of aid and to the benefits that the audit provides. The audit is also the only part of the COD Aid agreement that entails administrative costs, unlike input-based aid, which requires administrative inputs throughout the entire process (see figure 2.1).

In sum, the main requirements for the audit would be to invest in an identification number allocation system (or adopt an existing one), set up an electronic student database, develop tests, and manage the logistics for widespread and secure test administration, scoring, and reporting. The main effort of the audit would involve retesting a sample of schools, inspecting records, analyzing data, and generating easily understood reports.

Consequences: do the official reports pass or fail? Funders and recipients will expect the audit to confirm that the official reports are accurate. But it is very important for the agreement to specify precisely what constitutes accuracy and what happens if the audit detects problems. It should be kept in mind that the audit will be estimating only the total number of

The total cost of the audit could be as low as $250,000

assessed completers and their average test scores within a statistical margin of error. From our consultations with experts on this matter, we propose that the official report be considered accurate if the reported number of assessed completers and the average test scores are no more than 5 percent higher than the auditor's upper-bound estimate using a 95 percent level of statistical significance.

Once the official report passes the audit, the funder will make the payments specified in the contract. In our proposal, this means paying $20 per assessed completer up to the number of students who were enrolled in the last year of primary school in the first year of the COD Aid agreement (with the payment being phased out gradually over subsequent years) and an additional $200 per assessed completer for all students beyond the initial enrollment.

Consequences have to be specified for the possibility that the official reports overstate either the number of assessed completers or the average test score. In our proposal, the consequences are simple and direct. If the number of assessed completers is overstated, the funder will still make payments to the recipient but only according to the auditor's point estimate of assessed completers. If the test scores are overstated, the payment per assessed completer will be reduced by a factor proportional to overstatement. Structuring the penalties in this way lowers the stakes. The recipient is very likely to receive some payment, rather than all or nothing. But the penalty design gives the recipient an incentive to report the information as accurately as possible (see the appendix for further discussion of auditing and consequences).

Consequences: public audit reports create pressure for accurate reporting. The results of the audit will also be public information. The information must be made available in forms that are useful to the public and at the greatest level of disaggregation that is appropriate and feasible. The funder-recipient and funder-auditor contracts should specify what data will be public. For example, audit reports could list the names of schools whose retest numbers and scores diverged significantly from the official report. This aspect of the audit could encourage local accountability and stimulate attention to other aspects of schooling that cannot be captured in one or a few index numbers. The audit could also provide parents and civil society organizations with information about equity, quality of instruction, data manipulation, or unintended consequences, equipping them to pressure the education system to improve.

Provision for contingencies

COD Aid agreements are contracts that establish a payment for delivery of a particular good or service. As with any contract, it is impossible to foresee the future and anticipate all developments that might affect the parties' ability to fulfill their obligations. Such concerns can be addressed by designing an agreement that is robust in the face of predictable areas of disagreement, with contingencies for foreseeable events and arbitration for unforeseeable developments.

The proposed design for COD Aid to primary education incorporates features to make it robust. Choosing an indicator that is relatively easy to verify limits opportunities for manipulation and disagreement over payments. Measures to ensure transparency and public oversight also strengthen the agreement by reducing the likelihood that either party will try to renegotiate without good justification.

Contingencies are still necessary, however, for events beyond the recipient's control that could interfere with schooling or disrupt testing—such as major natural disasters or declines in the world price of an important export. While countries facing such crises may require additional aid, it is important for those funds to come through other channels. We think that appropriate contingencies could be included in the contract to allow rescheduling tests or delaying reports, but that payments under the COD Aid agreement should not otherwise be adjusted. Standard conditions for either party to withdraw from the contract are also necessary, as is a process for arbitration if irresolvable differences emerge. Recourse to arbitration should involve costs, so that it is not undertaken frivolously.

COD Aid is feasible

Our view, in short, is that the key features of a COD Aid agreement—payment for outcomes, hands-off funders and responsible recipients, independent verification with transparency and complementarity—can be captured in a robust contract reflecting a variety of specific country settings. We have shown how a particular indicator of progress—the number of additional assessed completers—can serve as the basis for a COD Aid agreement and how levels of payment, verification procedures, and contingencies could work in practice. To explore these ideas in greater detail and provide assistance for developing a COD Aid program, we have included term sheets for drafting the necessary contracts in the appendix. Chapter 4 considers issues related to funding and implementing the agreement once it has been negotiated and signed.

Conclusion: keeping it simple

This chapter has covered a great deal of detail, from base year enrollment and additional assessed completers to payment formulas, testing methods, and auditing requirements. The next chapter will discuss funding and implementation at a similar level of detail. This precision and specificity is essential to making a COD Aid agreement work. But specific need not mean complex. Indeed, in our review of lessons from previous efforts to reform foreign aid and our extensive consultations, we repeatedly returned

> **The key features of a COD Aid agreement can be captured in a robust contract**

to the imperative of keeping it simple. We conclude this chapter by underscoring four principles of simplicity:

- Choose a simple indicator.
- Choose a simple incentive.
- Support other ways of verifying progress.
- Use existing expertise.

Choose a simple indicator

In developing a COD Aid agreement, it is very easy for the discussion to begin with a simple indicator—which by definition can only approximate the true goal of a program—and move rapidly toward sophisticated indicators. Using sophisticated indicators can, however, undermine qualities of a COD Aid agreement that are critical to its success. For an agreement to be credible, the indicator must be clearly defined, focused, measurable with sufficient precision, and verifiable to reduce uncertainty over the deliverable. Credibility, in turn, is necessary for the agreement to create an incentive for the recipient. And unless the indicator can be easily explained to the public, it will be more difficult to hold funders and recipients accountable for compliance. This does not mean that a simplistic indicator should be chosen—it means that the tendency toward sophistication should be tempered by practicality and ease of understanding.

Choose a simple incentive

Another temptation in developing a COD Aid agreement is to take the concept of an incentive to extremes. The basic incentive is a payment for improvements in a measurable outcome. But if a single incentive is good, wouldn't many incentives be better? The temptation arises to add further and more complex incentives, such as rewarding complementary goals (improving teacher incentives, increasing the number of schools with a certain number of textbooks, introducing school autonomy, strengthening management information systems). It is also tempting to elaborate on the payment structure to closely reflect the amount of effort and expenditure required at different stages (such as successively increasing the per-student payment to address the increasing difficulty of reaching more marginalized children). As with choosing an indicator with the right balance of simplicity and sophistication, the incentive design must also find an appropriate balance. An incentive that involves different levels of payment for many related indicators is less effective than a single payment for progress toward a single outcome indicator because the added complexity necessarily diffuses managerial and political attention and reduces transparency to the public and civil society.

> Choosing an indicator with the right balance of simplicity and sophistication

Support other ways of verifying progress

While the COD Aid agreement itself needs to be simple, this does not preclude encouraging other agencies, civil society groups, or research institutions to monitor the full range of desirable outcomes. Our example focuses on a specific measurable indicator: the number of students completing school and taking a test. But even that indicator is only a proxy for the true objective: a well rounded education.

> While the COD Aid agreement needs to be simple, other agencies, civil society groups, or research institutions could monitor the full range of desirable outcomes

In countries with effective civil society organizations, groups can be encouraged to monitor inputs to learning and other aspects of schooling, such as teacher absenteeism, student attendance, and nuanced quality measures of classroom instruction and student achievement. Equipped with such information about a fuller range of indicators, civil society groups can exert pressure on the government to maintain and improve quality, and professional associations can engage in informed discussions with education policymakers. By encouraging the measurement and dissemination of other aspects of schooling, the COD Aid indicator can remain simple while civil society groups and other institutions provide more sophisticated oversight on aspects less easily reduced to single index numbers.

Use existing expertise

Funders and recipients have been working in most development sectors for decades, and a large body of knowledge and expertise has been generated through those experiences. These experts are an indispensable resource in solving the problems in designing a practical and useful COD Aid agreement. Indeed, the proposal described here is the outcome of many problem-solving sessions with international education experts over two years—and of background papers and notes commissioned to address particularly important issues such as testing, data systems, and auditing.[13]

Notes

1. Levine, Birdsall, and Ibrahim 2003.
2. This proposal comes from a background paper by Crouch and Mitchell (2008) commissioned for this project. Further arguments in favor of this indicator can be found in that background paper.
3. This is the definition used by the World Bank in its EdStats for the numerator in its primary completion rate. The United Nations Educational, Scientific, and Cultural Organization reports the same statistic but more transparently calls it gross intake ratio in the last grade of primary. See also Bruns, Mingat, and Rakotomalala (2003), p. 40.
4. This section draws heavily on a background paper by Lockheed (2008) commissioned for this project.
5. Lockheed 2008; Holland and Rubin 1982; Linn 2005.

6. Available international and regional tests include the Organisation for Economic Co-operation and Development's Programme for International Student Assessment or the Southern African Consortium for Monitoring Educational Quality.

7. Such organizations include Trends in International Mathematics and Science Study, Progress in International Reading Literacy Study, and Programme d'Analyse des Systèmes Educatifs de la CONFEMEN.

8. Drawn from Crouch and Mitchell (2008).

9. Lockheed 2008.

10. This section draws directly from and extensively quotes a background paper by Crouch and Mitchell (2008) commissioned for this project.

11. See box 7.1 for an example of how relying on the recipient to report progress can create problems.

12. The sample must be truly random, such as including schools that are difficult to reach because of distance, conflicts, or transportation difficulties. Otherwise, there would be a temptation to manipulate results in schools unlikely to be visited.

13. A list of these background papers and notes is available on CGD's website at www.cgdev.org/section/initiatives/_active/codaid/papers_and_resources.

Applying COD Aid to primary education: funding and implementation

The previous chapter described many aspects of a Cash on Delivery Aid (COD Aid) agreement for increasing primary school completion. This chapter addresses the issues that are apt to arise regarding funding and implementing such a program. We discuss the possible financial arrangements for a COD Aid agreement, ways to help funders fulfill long-term COD Aid commitments, and provisions to ensure that COD Aid is additional to other forms of foreign aid. We then turn to potential institutional structures for COD Aid and explore how the many different actors—bilateral aid agencies, multilateral banks, private foundations—could be involved.

Funding a COD Aid Agreement

Who are the possible funders of COD Aid programs? One of the attractive aspects of COD Aid is that many different types of funders may be interested in and capable of participating: private foundations, national and international nongovernmental organizations, as well as official bilateral and multilateral agencies. It should be underscored that in a COD Aid agreement, a funder can be distinguished from an implementing agency, where the latter might be a separate entity with responsibility for negotiating the contract, arranging the audit, and disbursing funds. For example, a private foundation might wish to join in funding an ongoing COD Aid program while delegating all implementation functions to a governmental aid agency with in-country negotiating experience and fiduciary capacity.

Financial arrangements and long-term commitments

One of the problems funders face, especially public funders, is that their budget cycles often preclude long term commitments like the one envisioned

Arranging
a binding
commitment
to provide a
variable amount
of funding over
five years can
be a daunting
challenge

for COD Aid. Arranging a binding commitment to provide a variable amount of funding over five years can be a daunting challenge for funding bureaucracies. But it can be done. For example, the United States has established five-year compacts with recipients of Millennium Challenge Account funds through an arrangement with Congress that allows money to be spent outside the fiscal year in which it is allocated. The U.K. Department for International Development also has 10-year partnership agreements with recipients. These provide greater certainty about long-term funding. Given the high cost to recipients of the unpredictability of aid, longer term arrangements for aid are sorely needed. The bureaucratic problems are worth solving to make aid work better.[1]

For COD Aid, other solutions to bureaucratic rigidities are available. For example, funds could be placed in escrow based on projected disbursements and modified as experience with the program unfolds. The rules for the escrow fund could specify that unused money would remain in escrow for future years if it appears that the recipient will make progress on the shared goal. Rules for the escrow account could also establish the conditions for releasing funds to other recipients joining the COD Aid program. They might also provide explicit steps for transferring funds to other development purposes, or to global public goods such as agricultural or health research, when recipients fail to make progress on agreed goals.

Another approach would treat the COD Aid funds as prize money to be completely disbursed each year. In this case, the per-student amount would vary depending on the total number of additional assessed completers in a pool of participating countries. Thus, countries would be implicitly competing to perform better than their peers and thereby receive a larger share of the prize money (see box 2.2).

Additionality: giving with one hand and taking with the other?

A concern frequently expressed in our consultations is that COD Aid could displace other forms of foreign aid. This would occur if funders were to decide unilaterally after an agreement is signed to reduce funding to the country's education sector for each dollar of COD Aid disbursed. Indeed, there is no way to absolutely guarantee that a funder will not use the existence of COD Aid as an excuse to reduce other forms of foreign aid. We believe this is not a grave concern for two reasons. First, as we explained above, the last decade has seen a tremendous interest in scaling up foreign aid. With the recent international economic downturn, the likelihood of near-term increases in aid has declined. Even so, the broad secular decline that occurred in the 1990s after the end of the Cold War is unlikely, if only because foreign aid is more readily seen as a strategic and security tool in an age of interdependence. Second, funders are showing more interest in rewarding well performing countries. To reduce foreign aid programs to a country accelerating progress in education would be contrary to this increasingly important tenet of foreign aid.

Although it is not possible to guarantee that COD Aid would be additional to existing foreign aid, it is possible to include an explicit contract provision that funders at least abide by all existing foreign aid commitments to the recipients. This would be an enforceable provision with real consequences because canceling of previously approved education grants would violate other contractual commitments. While the contract could also commit the funder to make COD Aid additional to future programmed assistance or expectations about future educational programs, any provisions for the future would be enforceable only through moral suasion and the court of public opinion.

If COD Aid were tried and shown to be effective at promoting better development outcomes with low transaction costs, both funders and recipients might actually prefer to expand its role in foreign aid, and the concern about additionality would be irrelevant. Once funders (public and private, national and multilateral) and recipient countries have more experience with COD Aid, they will see its strengths and weaknesses and can judge whether it is more or less effective than other forms of foreign aid. Both parties can then also judge whether it works better as a complement to existing forms of aid or can stand on its own. They could then jointly make informed choices about the extent to which COD Aid should be additional to or replace other forms of aid.

Loans and grants

Thus far we have discussed COD Aid in its most direct form: a funder and recipient agree on a shared goal, the recipient makes progress, the progress is verified, and the funder pays for progress. Other arrangements are possible and could offer significant advantages and flexibility.

One variation on a COD Aid agreement would include the involvement of three parties: a lender (which could be a commercial bank or a multilateral development bank); the borrower-recipient; and a grantor (which could be a private foundation or other organization).[2]

In this variant, all three parties would be involved in negotiations and come to a shared agreement on the standard components of any COD Aid contract: a fixed payment per unit of progress, a way to measure progress, and a mechanism for third-party verification. In this variant, the three parties would also estimate the likely flow of COD Aid payments under mutually agreed future scenarios of progress. The borrower-recipient would then borrow funds from the lender in proportion to the anticipated COD Aid payments and use those funds to invest in activities that the borrower-recipient has chosen to achieve progress. As with progress measured and verified, the actual COD Aid payments would be calculated. The grantor would then make payments in that amount directly to the lender, paying back the loan.

> It is possible to include an explicit contract provision that funders at least abide by all existing foreign aid commitments

If the borrower-recipient were to progress more swiftly than anticipated, the loan would be paid off more quickly, and all future payments under the agreement would go directly to the borrower-recipient. If the borrower-recipient were less successful than expected, the loan would be paid off more slowly. What if the borrower-recipient were to fail completely to make progress? This is an important risk and would leave the borrower-recipient in debt for funds it had applied ineffectually. While this is certainly not the most desirable outcome, it is no different from what happens whenever a country borrows money for development projects and fails to achieve its aims. For example, when a developing country government borrows money to implement a traditional primary education program, it has to repay that loan regardless of whether it succeeds in educating children. Pairing such a loan with a COD Aid grantor's promise to pay down the loan in proportion to success creates the opportunity to buy down that debt, a stronger incentive to succeed, and freer ability to use funds according to the borrower-recipient's own strategies.

This concept of buying down loans for successful programs is not unique to COD Aid. Indeed, something like it is already in operation. Under a program started in 2003, governments can borrow from the World Bank to implement polio eradication programs. These loans are channeled through the International Development Association (IDA), the World Bank's soft-loan arm for the poorest countries. If the polio eradication programs are implemented successfully, a partnership involving the Bill and Melinda Gates Foundation and Rotary International/United Nations Foundation will buy down the country's IDA loan. Because of the generous loan terms, each grant dollar unlocks $2.50–$3.00 for affected countries to fight polio. To fund the buy-downs, the partnership has established a trust fund with $25 million from the Gates Foundation and $25 million from Rotary International/UN Foundation. This $50 million investment will buy down $120–$140 million in World Bank IDA loans. In this way, developing countries can mobilize what ultimately becomes grant funding to eradicate polio, and thus contribute beyond their national borders to the global campaign to eliminate polio transmission worldwide.

With this type of three-way agreement within a COD Aid project, it would have advantages for each of the three parties. The borrower-recipient would gain access to upfront funding for necessary investments to make progress while continuing to have complete discretion over how to use those funds (unlike standard loans or traditional development programs). If the borrower-recipient makes good progress, it would not pay the loan back, though it would bear the risk of failure if no progress were made. The lender would gain assurance that the loans would be used well and repaid, due to the distinctive features of COD Aid (focus on outcome, recipient responsibility, verification of progress, and transparency) as well as the involvement of the grantor. And the grantor would gain

The concept of buying down loans for successful programs is not unique to COD Aid

greater confidence that the borrower-recipient would have the up front resources to make progress, while also leveraging funding from large lending institutions.

> The COD Aid agreement could be available as an open contract

Should financing stop if an exogenous adverse event blocks progress?
An important feature of the COD Aid agreement is to provide a firm incentive for the recipient to make progress, but outcomes depend on factors both in and outside the control of the recipient. Thus, the question arises: is it fair for a recipient to have to forgo an expected COD Aid payment because of a sharp reduction in national income due to adverse weather or a shift in international terms of trade reduces public expenditures or the ability of households to send their children to school?

While it is appropriate for other countries to provide additional assistance to countries facing such adverse shocks, the COD Aid agreement should not be modified to address this need. The COD Aid agreement does cover contingencies, but they should focus on factors that interfere with measuring progress. For example, it is appropriate for the contract to include provisions to address external factors (such as weather) that interfere with applying the annual test or collecting administrative data, so long as these factors are clearly beyond the recipient's control. In such cases, the contract could permit delays in applying tests or submitting reports. Similarly, the contract should include provisions for addressing any discrepancies between government reports of outcomes and the auditor's estimates. By contrast, the agreement should not include a provision that permits COD Aid payments to be based on anything other than verified progress in the number of children completing primary school. Any contingencies that weaken the link between payment for and delivery of the outcome also weaken the incentive that the COD Aid agreement is meant to create.

Implementation: who and how?
In the first COD Aid agreements, a small number of recipient countries is likely to be involved in negotiating the arrangement. Once funders and recipients have experience with this new modality, an institutional arrangement could be adopted that allows the COD Aid agreement to be available as an open contract. Funders and recipients would negotiate a single agreement that would become a standing offer for any eligible recipient to join. Funders, whether private or public, would put money forward for any country interested in participating.

An open contract is attractive for several reasons. First, it would reduce administrative costs, because further negotiations would be unnecessary. Second, it would increase transparency through simplicity and uniformity. And third, it would encourage self-selection of countries for which the terms would be most attractive (for example, a fixed payment of $200 per additional assessed completer would be of much greater interest to low-income than middle-income countries). An open contract would require, in addition, some provisions to limit the funders' exposure, either by restricting the contract to a specific number of countries or establishing a maximum payout.

While it is possible to develop a COD Aid agreement for reaching universal primary schooling as an independent initiative, the international community already has institutions and initiatives that could support or even administer a COD Aid arrangement. The United Nations Educational, Scientific, and Cultural Organization, the Fast Track Initiative for Education, multilateral development banks, bilateral aid agencies, and major private foundations engaged in efforts to expand primary schooling all have their own well established administrative and technical capacities. Before creating an additional independent initiative, it would be advisable to explore opportunities for working through existing institutions.

In our discussions, we identified at least three basic ways to implement a COD Aid agreement for primary education: one or more bilateral agencies participate both as funder and as implementing agency; a multilateral agency negotiates and manages the programs with its own or other resources; and an existing multilateral initiative that included the education sector incorporates COD Aid.

One or more bilateral agencies. One or more bilateral agencies could offer COD Aid as a pilot in multiple countries. For example, the European Commission could incorporate a COD Aid component into its Millennium Development Goal contracts. The Millennium Challenge Corporation could complement its threshold programs or compacts with COD Aid funding for countries that fail its education indicator.

A multilateral agency. A multilateral agency such as the World Bank or a regional development bank could provide the framework and logistical support for a COD Aid agreement. The agency would negotiate the contract with potential recipients, support the development of tests, contract and supervise the auditor, disburse funds, and contract an evaluation of the arrangement. Bilateral agencies, private foundations, and individual philanthropists could contribute to the fund managed by this agency.

A multilateral initiative in the education sector. COD Aid could be part of an existing multilateral initiative in the education sector. In particular, the Fast Track Initiative for Education is a promising institutional base for a COD Aid initiative. Established in 2002, it brings together bilateral and multilateral donors that have committed to provide funding to any country with a strong plan to scale up education. It works in two ways. First, it streamlines vetting of country policies, so funders do this once as a group instead of draining recipient and funder resources with duplicative processes.

Second, it pools funding from many sources, to support countries in expanding primary education.

The members of the Fast Track Initiative could create a special Innovation Fund separate from the Education Program Development Fund and Catalytic Fund. Contributions to this new fund would be voluntary, and the use of its resources would be flexible enough to experiment with innovations like COD Aid.[3] The Fast Track Initiative and its members could then offer a COD Aid agreement to a number of recipients, relying on the initiative's existing contacts, reviews of education sector plans, and financial administration.

Public-private partnership for progress. In each of the cases above, agreements can be structured so that both public and private funders could contribute. Particularly in arrangements involving multilateral agencies and initiatives, it should be possible to establish funds for COD Aid into which private money could be contributed. Putting the institutional structure in place would allow private contributors to support progress in education without the administrative costs and commitment of establishing operations in each country. Private funders would also benefit from the low risk of this approach: if no progress is achieved, no funds are spent.

Audit and arbitration

The role of third parties in the COD Aid agreement is critical to its success, particularly auditing the reported progress measure and arbitrating any eventual disagreements over implementing the contract.

To verify the outcome measure, implementation of the COD Aid agreement requires that the funder and recipient agree on a pool of mutually acceptable agents (chapter 3). The funder then selects and hires one of those agents to conduct retests at a randomly selected sample of schools and to assess the validity of administrative reports from those schools.

The COD Aid agreement also requires a further set of independent agents to arbitrate when disagreements arise over the implementation of the contract. Disagreements can occur over any number of things—the technical quality of the recipient's reporting, the auditor's reports, the quality of the test, the calculation of payments, unanticipated changes in public education policy. Issues not foreseen cannot be incorporated in the COD Aid agreement and thus require some form of binding arbitration to resolve.

To address this possibility, a COD Aid agreement could include a procedure to establish an arbitration committee. If a disagreement were to arise, the recipient and funder would agree on a group of people to serve on such a committee. It might comprise, say, five internationally respected individuals who are not citizens of the countries involved in the dispute and who have relevant expertise in law, education, finance, or

> Agreements can be structured so that both public and private funders could contribute

the social sciences. Once the committee is empaneled, the funder and recipient would make their cases to the committee and be required to abide by its final decision. The contract would also specify a range of potential remedies available to the committee (such as maximum financial penalties, ability to dissolve the agreement). Recourse to the arbitration procedure should involve costs so that it is not frivolous; for example, the losing party might have to pay the costs of the arbitration.

Hands-off does not preclude engagement

While the COD Aid agreement explicitly delinks a funder's contribution of money from its contribution of expertise, this by no means prohibits the funder from engaging substantively with the recipient. The delinking means, however, that a funder's engagement with the recipient on discussions of strategy or policy is at the recipient's request. Whatever the technical assistance or policy dialogue, it will be more meaningful when clearly demand-driven. The value of any technical support will have to be evident to the recipient rather than merely attached as a condition for receiving funds.

In our consultations on applying COD Aid to the education sector, many education specialists within funding institutions were reluctant to embrace the new aid modality because it seemed to eliminate their engagement with recipients. Their views often changed when they understood that linking aid to outcomes would give them an opportunity to engage in discussions with recipient governments about the best way to educate students and solve problems rather than negotiate over the purchasing and monitoring of specific inputs.

In sum, the challenges of implementing and financing a COD Aid agreement are quite surmountable, and many of the challenges have already been addressed by other aid modalities. Several countries have found ways to make long-term financial aid commitments that exceed their internal budget cycles. Private foundations have established mechanisms for buying down development loans. And many international contracts contain provisions for independent arbitration. The model contract provided in the appendix incorporates these already established solutions to some of the challenges anticipated in implementing a COD Aid agreement.

Notes

1. Eifert and Gelb 2005; Kharas 2008.
2. The lender and grantor could be the same organization, but for exposition, it helps to think of them separately.
3. These ideas have been discussed with Fast Track Initiative staff, and in principle are consistent with the initiatives' system.

Learning what works:
the research challenge

Cash on Delivery Aid (COD Aid) is a new approach to foreign assistance that could have a profound impact on the practices, commitments, and strategies of both funders and recipients. If COD Aid were implemented, funders would pay only for results—not for inputs, not for promises. Recipients would have complete responsibility for progress—for the design and execution of programs, and for their ultimate success or failure. COD Aid thus changes the dynamics of incentives, control, and accountability for all the major players in a foreign aid agreement.

Undertaking such a significant innovation in foreign aid without documenting and evaluating the experience would be irresponsible. Indeed, a COD Aid program provides many opportunities to better understand what works in foreign aid. Merely knowing whether progress toward a goal was achieved will not tell us whether COD Aid was essential to that progress. Just knowing that progress was slow will not tell us the cause—whether the underlying concept of COD Aid, the contract for a particular COD Aid program, the recipient's chosen policies and strategies, or external factors. Each COD Aid initiative is an opportunity to learn from experience and to design better policies for transferring aid and better programs for advancing specific development goals.

COD Aid provides an opportunity to learn about the influence of its distinctive incentive structures on the decisions and practices of both funders and recipients. Does COD Aid's emphasis on verified outcomes, recipient discretion, and transparency help funders and recipients align their interests? Does it alter relationships of accountability between funders and their constituents, between recipients and their constituents, and between funders and recipient governments? Does it improve the flow of foreign aid

Design the research framework simultaneously with the negotiation and design of the COD Aid agreement

through lower administrative costs, greater coordination among funders, or more consistent and predictable funding streams? Does it release more resources for recipient progress, whether in the form of freedom to explore innovative strategies rather than fulfilling funder requirements, or greater involvement and commitment from a civil society that has more information for holding officials accountable?

Systematically addressing this range of potential research questions is better achieved by designing the research framework simultaneously with the negotiation and design of the COD Aid agreement itself. This chapter explores the multiple purposes and levels of research with any COD Aid program and further research questions to explore usefully. It then reviews some methodological issues to ensure that the research is rigorous and systematic, discussing the process approach as a particularly relevant mode of research. The chapter closes with some practical suggestions for the composition and qualifications of the research team.

Purpose of the research

The main purpose of the research that should accompany any COD Aid initiative is to assess whether it is an effective way to use foreign aid to achieve development goals. Answering this question requires an explicit distinction between two levels of analysis: how the COD Aid approach affects funder and recipient behaviors and how the recipient's resulting actions affect actual outcomes (here, increased schooling and learning). The relationship between these two distinct levels of analysis is illustrated in figure 5.1.

The northwest box of the figure displays the impact of the COD Aid agreement on funder and recipient actions—the causal link of interest in determining whether COD Aid is more effective than other forms of foreign aid. Funders and recipients would be expected to respond to the COD Aid agreement by reorganizing institutions, changing policies, realigning political interest groups, reallocating funding, or expanding investments. Since we know something of the nature of the agreement and the participating actors, it is possible to outline a basic methodology for this first level of research and analysis.

The second level, illustrated in the southeast box, addresses the link between the recipient's actions and the outcome—that is, between changes in government policies and educational outcomes. Appropriate methods for analyzing this second level cannot be identified until the recipient chooses how to respond to the challenge posed by the COD Aid agreement. Because research for this level of analysis cannot be designed until after the recipient chooses strategies for accelerating progress, it is critical to establish a mechanism for assessing the research opportunities the recipient's actions presents. For example, the funder and recipient could establish a working group—at

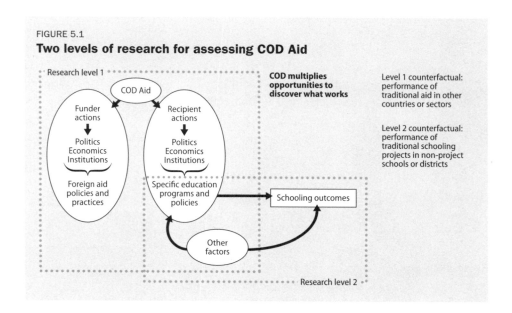

FIGURE 5.1

Two levels of research for assessing COD Aid

a minimum to include representatives of the funder, the recipient, and the group researching the first level of analysis—to monitor the country's responses and propose additional evaluations or research when appropriate in light of a new intervention.

In some cases, the recipient might respond with programs that can be tested in a small number of schools or introduced at different times across the country. Such initiatives include school feeding programs, special payments to induce teachers to stay in rural areas, conditional cash transfers to encourage parents to keep their daughters in school, improvements in infrastructure, greater autonomy for schools, changes in personnel management, and linking managerial promotions to performance indicators. For these kinds of initiatives, the ability to apply the intervention in one place and not in another makes it easier to establish a counterfactual in the impact evaluation design and generate strong evidence on how and why the programs achieved what they did.

In other cases, government action in response to the COD Aid agreement might be national and indivisible. For example, it might negotiate a new relationship with a national teachers' union, establish an interministerial working group to assess policies across sectors that affect education, or appoint a new minister of education with different qualifications. In these cases, it may be more difficult to identify appropriate counterfactuals. The scope for good quantitative analyses of government programs, however, has been shown to be wider than previously believed, as demonstrated by a new generation of impact evaluations, and should not be dismissed without concerted effort.[1]

Monitor the country's responses and propose additional evaluations or research when appropriate in light of a new intervention

Try the COD Aid approach in a few places and then carefully and rigorously assess the results

The distinction between the two levels of analysis is significant. The success of COD Aid (relative to other forms of foreign aid) is not the same thing as the success of the recipient's education programs. The COD Aid approach could be very successful in inducing the funder and recipient to change their behavior and undertake promising innovations that, for any number of reasons, fail to accelerate the expansion of primary education. Similarly, primary education might expand more rapidly for reasons unrelated to COD Aid. The separation of an evaluation of COD Aid from an evaluation of specific policy innovations introduced by the recipient must be maintained in the research design. Box 5.1 summarizes the research strategies appropriate to the two levels of analysis.

The rest of this chapter addresses primarily the first level of analysis, with greater emphasis on the response of the recipient government. The focus is on the recipient government because that is where the underlying premise of the COD Aid approach can be tested directly: does introducing an incentive tied to outcomes encourage the recipient to innovate in pursuit of improved outcomes? How the agreement affects the behavior of funders is also addressed, because one of the objectives of introducing COD Aid is to facilitate fulfillment of the commitments in the 2005 Paris Declaration. These include recipient ownership, alignment of incentives, coordination among donors, and the predictability of aid flows. We fully recognize that governments are not monolithic and that competing interests, intertemporal considerations, and

BOX 5.1

Summary of research strategies at two levels of analysis

The research strategy at the first level should include collection and analysis of baseline information on both the funder and recipient. For the funder, this entails studying its prior experience with foreign aid, the context for developing its foreign aid programs, its relation to other funders, and very importantly its relationship with recipients. This contextual information is also important to assess the generalizability of the findings. The first funder or funders to enter into a COD Aid agreement may not be typical of other funders, given their demonstrated willingness to experiment with a new aid modality.

For the recipient, baseline information includes political economy, bureaucratic relationships, sectoral governance, interactions with aid bureaucracies, expenditures by different levels of government on schooling, past and current aid-financed expenditures, school system issues (teachers, unions, absenteeism), government structure (allocations between different levels of government, relation of executive and legislature), and accountability relationships.

This baseline information is followed by process monitoring and tracing over the period of the funder-recipient contract (five years) and developing quasi counterfactuals in the form of systematic assessments of how other aid modalities are operating in similar settings. Attention to the incentives and the responses they elicit would be a major emphasis of those comparisons.

historical factors complicate predicting the behavior of either funders or recipients. This is exactly why it is essential to try the COD Aid approach in a few places and then to carefully and rigorously assess the results.

The research strategy at the second level depends on whether the recipient government decides to undertake new interventions and is willing to implement them in a way that permits rigorous evaluation. More governments are interested and willing to assess the impact of interventions through programs that compare outcomes across population groups, taking advantage of differences in implementation across regions or over time. It is commonly agreed that impact evaluations are likely to generate better quality evidence if they accompany a program from its earliest stage of development.

The principal-agent model and the model of change

Chapter 1 described a core problem underlying the relationship between any funder and any recipient in the principal-agent model. The funder and the recipient share an interest in some development goal that provides the basis for foreign aid, but they also have independent interests that are not aligned. Attending to the interplay of shared and divergent interests generates important questions and hypotheses to guide the investigation. The example of foreign aid for education can be examined within the framework of the principal-agent model—recognizing, of course, that any model necessarily simplifies reality and will be useful only insofar as it improves the rigor of empirical analysis and frames conclusions that are relevant to public policy.

Funder behavior

The starting assumption is that the funder (or principal to the contract) wants to see more children educated and is willing to transfer resources to the recipient (or agent) to get that job done. The funder may have other objectives as well. It may want to support developing countries with good diplomatic relations or cultural or linguistic ties. It may also seek increased demand for its goods and services (tied aid). For private philanthropies, another objective may be to generate visibility for their causes to leverage their own contributions. Some funders may be highly concerned about their reputations and particularly careful to avoid the waste or theft of the funds they provide. Any of these divergent objectives could induce the funder to interfere in the way aid money is used. The overarching question for this research would be whether COD Aid limits the tendency for funders to interfere with the recipient's autonomy.

Within the framework of the principal-agent model, the following questions arise:

- With the focus on verified outcomes, does the funder reduce the resources allocated to monitor inputs, compared with other funders, or its own past behavior?

> A core problem underlying the relationship between any funder and any recipient in the principal-agent model

- Do the funder's administrative costs fall relative to its other forms of aid?
- With transfers linked to verified outcomes, does the funder focus more on reporting of outcomes to their own constituents than other funders or than it did in the past?
- Once the COD Aid agreement is started with one recipient, does the funder try the COD approach elsewhere? Do other funders become interested and try COD Aid?
- Does the COD Aid approach improve recipient ownership, alignment of incentives between funder and recipient, and coordination with other funders?

Recipient behavior

The recipient (agent) also has objectives besides the one shared directly with the funder. It may seek to minimize political difficulties with unions and opposition parties, to ensure ethnically diverse children all learn the national language, to reward provincial politicians in particular districts, or to extend the textbook contract of a supporter. Furthermore, the recipient cannot be treated as a unitary entity. The recipient is a composite of many actors who give different weights to the range of objectives, with expanding education as only one. The various actors on the recipient side can also be presumed to have more information than the funder about their relationships to each other and their influence on other actors in their political or social system, whose behavior will advance or deter progress toward the agreed goal.

The implicit model of change is that, because COD Aid payments are linked to achieved and verified outcomes, the recipient will give greater weight to schooling progress relative to its other objectives. Given the complex character of the recipient, it might be better to think of the COD Aid agreement as changing the weight given to schooling by some actors and increasing the leverage of actors who have a strong interest in reaching universal primary completion. A key aspect of this research is to ascertain whether the COD Aid approach significantly changes the political-economy of policy formation—by modifying institutions, shifting power, or changing accountability relationships at the government level—and whether those changes improve the provision of education.

The recipient has objectives besides the one shared directly with the funder

Current theories of development focus on institutions and governance. Many aid critics have expressed concern that the influence of traditional aid modalities on institutions and governance can be harmful. The research proposed here would ascertain whether similar problems arise with COD Aid or whether our expectation that COD Aid would actually improve institutions and governance is realized.

Method

The methodology for the research accompanying the COD Aid agreement should be as rigorous and systematic as possible as to substantially confirm three fundamental and related issues: attribution, causation, and external validity. The relevant questions can be articulated as follows.

- On attribution, what is the net impact of the COD Aid agreement?
- On causation, through what mechanisms does the COD Aid agreement cause that net impact?
- On external validity, to what extent can the answers to the first two questions be generalized to other contexts?

> A process approach analyzes how strategic decisions advance or hinder a reform initiative

The unit of analysis for this research is the COD Aid agreement between the funder and the recipient. As COD Aid begins to be introduced, the initial number of observations will be limited to one or a few cases. Statistical methods that rely on a large number of observations relative to the variables being studied will therefore be unsuitable. Nonetheless, researchers should still begin by looking for ways to use statistical comparisons—say, by taking advantage of differences across subnational governments in a large country. The goal is to generate quantitative evidence that can plausibly attribute changes in schooling to the COD Aid agreement.

Research methods other than statistical approaches can also provide reliable evidence on attribution, causality, and external validity if they are conducted systematically and rigorously. Comparisons across countries, provinces, or sectors will be significant sources of information, as will careful longitudinal analyses. In particular, researchers are most likely to learn about the actual conditions and the dynamic responses of organizations through a process approach.

A process approach

A process approach traces events in context and analyzes how strategic decisions advance or hinder a reform initiative.[2] It identifies the path from idea to policy proposal and then to a place on the policy agenda. The next steps to be traced are program design, including input from and negotiations among various actors, then approval and adjustments. Implementation—or failure to implement—is the next phase of the path. The kinds of questions relevant in a process approach include:

- Who took the initiative to set up a meeting, to write a policy proposal, to suggest a change, and so on?
- Who was involved in this discussion?
- When was the decision made to take a particular action?
- Why was that decision made rather than another one?
- What followed?

The answers to these questions can be turned into a meaningful narrative of what happened and why. This narrative can be tested against alternative explanations by

Such research focuses on political processes embedded in historical and cultural contexts

comparing it with accounts of what happened in other countries, in other sectors, or in other time periods. To be complete and rigorous, the narrative needs to be tested against independent data on expenditures, inputs, outputs, and especially outcomes.

Experience with conducting such research provides four practical lessons. First, researchers need to establish a complete baseline, including initial data on expenditures, inputs, outputs, and outcomes. The baseline should also include relevant information about the political and institutional features of the country and its education system. In addition, the research should establish a baseline of initial expectations about the new initiative. This requires interviews prior to implementation of the COD Aid agreement with important actors in the policy process, such as the minister of education, the minister of finance, various vice-ministers, lead administrators, the technical and bureaucratic units formulating policy and regulations, the leadership of the teachers' unions, and even a small sample of teachers. The interviews should be open-ended—to explore the actors' understanding of and expectations about the initiative. Questions at this stage might include: Do you think the COD Aid agreement is a good way to improve education? Does it seem feasible to you? What problems would you expect this approach to encounter? How would you anticipate your government, staff, and citizens to respond to this new initiative? This kind of research will provide valuable information on the goals, motivations, and understandings of key actors at the start, as well as insights into their subsequent actions. It might also provide information on how the way a COD Aid initiative is introduced influences initial expectations and the understanding of incentives.

Second, because such research focuses on political processes embedded in historical and cultural contexts, researchers must be well acquainted with the country. This does not mean that researchers must be from the country, but they should be very familiar with its general political economy, institutions, and history.

Third, a process approach requires that researchers have access to decisionmakers and implementers. Such access should be negotiated in advance of the program, or the researcher should have enough prior credibility and connections in the country to ensure access. Often, academics in a country have a good appreciation of the general political economy and the specific policy area and can be valuable researchers and informants. Technical teams that work on policy design in particular ministries may also be good informants, because they have observed many local policy initiatives move from the design through the implementation.

Fourth, judgments about attribution and insights into causality will be more convincing if comparisons are with analogous situations without a COD Aid agreement. Such situations may be found in the country's recent history, in parallel programs within the same sector (say, in secondary or tertiary education rather than primary education), simultaneously in other sectors (such as health or welfare programs), or in the same subsector in another very similar country. In each case, researchers would have to document how the comparator is similar to and different from the COD Aid agreement for assessing the internal and external validity of any conclusions derived from the comparison.

Such comparative work entails isolating one or two other relevant policy reform initiatives and then, through interviews with the principal actors and review of relevant documents, reconstructing the process of policymaking and policy implementation. Relevant tasks are identifying who was involved in the earlier initiatives, who made the important decisions, with whom they worked and consulted, what actions they took, what procedures they observed, and how they sought to manage opposition, mobilize support, and encourage effective implementation. Such comparisons provide a basis for demonstrating that the COD Aid agreement generated a distinct policy process.

In the education example, a comparative case approach might make it possible to test such hypotheses as:

- The COD Aid agreement encouraged the government to involve ministries from outside the education sector (finance, infrastructure, health) in developing the strategy for reaching education targets.
- The COD Aid agreement encouraged the government to implement institutional changes, such as increasing autonomy for schools or decentralizing budget and disbursement authority.
- The COD Aid agreement encouraged the government to reform personnel management, such as different forms of evaluation, amount of pay, pay incentives, and new modes of teacher training and support.
- The COD Aid agreement encouraged the government to improve administrative information systems, data collection, and analysis.
- As a result of published test results, public attention focused on districts or groups of students whose learning outcomes were lowest and linked these outcomes to budget decisions or policy choices at the national or state level.
- As a result of the publication of data, civil society organizations engaged at the grassroots level, for example, by designing and disseminating school report cards.
- The COD Aid agreement encouraged the government to request technical assistance—and, if so, of what kind?
- The COD Aid agreement encouraged the funder to relate differently with the recipient country—and, if so, in what ways?
- The COD Aid agreement led to negative consequences, such as lower standards for completion or interference with completion data.

> Researchers would have to document how the comparator is similar to and different from the COD Aid agreement

> **The implementation phase will be the most difficult part of the process to trace**

Process tracing can then follow the four initial steps outlined here—collecting the baseline data along with interviews regarding expectations, researching the context, ensuring access to key actors, and establishing one or more comparative cases. Researchers would acquire information about who is involved in discussions, what decisions are made in what arenas, how information is being conveyed, and a variety of other process-related issues that would make it possible to reconstruct the unfolding of the reform initiative.

This kind of information is best acquired through interviews with important actors in the process. Researchers would need access to these individuals and should be in contact with them frequently to monitor the process as it occurs. Interviews with several different actors will provide multiple perspectives on events and should be checked against documentation, data, and events to ensure the validity, coherence, and plausibility of the individual accounts.

The implementation phase will be the most difficult part of the process to trace. Effective implementation of education policies involves many actors (administrators, teachers, teachers' unions, teacher training institutions) at many different levels (national government, state and local government, school district, schools, classrooms, communities). Any of these actors at any of these levels can be responsible for how policy intent is or is not translated into actions and outcomes.

To study the implementation of a policy, researchers may need to adopt distinct methodologies. They should continue to follow the implementation process at each level—for example, from the central government, to a subnational government, to a program office, to school directors, to teachers, and finally to community engagement. In addition, surveys of school directors and teachers should be conducted at the beginning and end of the study. Surveys would reveal how these actors understood and acted on their understanding of the new education strategy, as well as how their attitudes and behaviors changed over the course of the program.

The research at this stage properly focuses on policy actors at the center who make decisions and determine how policy changes are introduced and implemented. Other stages of the research will address how stakeholders are affected by new policies and programs. While in some situations stakeholders may also have a policy role, they often do not. In education, children and parents are key stakeholders, yet in many countries they are absent from the policy process. Individual teachers are also stakeholders but not necessarily actors in the policy process, while teachers' unions may be both stakeholders and actors. At this stage, research rightly examines the decisions and actions of those with the leverage and capacity to shape the policy process, while also noting those absent from the table when important decisions are made and how this reflects existing power relationships.

A final caveat is in order regarding extrapolation from the first few COD cases. Researchers have documented ways that pilot experiences differ from subsequent efforts to replicate a program. Early experiences are likely to attract countries more comfortable with innovations or having a greater urgency to make progress. Early experiences are also likely to get much more managerial attention and staff time than subsequent efforts. Even the existence of a sophisticated research project, with key actors being contacted from time to time by external figures, may influence the course of events. Any conclusions on the generalizability of COD Aid will have to be qualified by this potential source of bias.

> In sum, a process approach with comparative material is the most promising

In sum, a process approach with comparative material is the most promising method for addressing the attribution, causation, and external validity of the net impact of the COD Aid agreement. This approach requires researchers to:

- Thoroughly investigate and understand the context.
- Have easy and informal access to key actors.
- Document and analyze one or more relevant comparative cases.
- Conduct initial interviews regarding expectations with key actors.
- Trace processes and the course of events during implementation through interviews and surveys.
- Analyze data on expenditures, inputs, outputs, and outcomes.

Team qualifications

The research team conducting this research should be properly qualified. First, the team needs experience in analyzing policy reforms, probably with expertise in political science, sociology, economics, and international relations. Second, the team should be knowledgeable about the history, institutions, and debates on foreign aid. Third, the team needs a thorough understanding of the recipient history, politics, society, and institutions. Finally, the team has to be well regarded domestically so that it can maintain access to policymakers and other actors—and well regarded internationally so that its findings will be credible.

For almost any COD Aid agreement, the composition of the research team is likely to be stronger if it includes both foreign and domestic researchers. Foreign researchers can bring important perspectives and experiences from investigations in other contexts. Domestic researchers bring important insights and experience from their in-depth knowledge of their country.

In presenting this proposal for COD Aid, we have taken the time to detail the research component because we accord it great significance. It would be irresponsible to undertake such a profound innovation as COD Aid aims to be without carefully preparing to evaluate its impact. And making progress and achieving outcomes are the whole point of this proposed reform—not satisfying reporting requirements, maintaining a certain mix of inputs, or meeting ancillary objectives. A key ingredient to achieving outcomes is taking advantage of every opportunity to learn what works and how.

Notes

1. See Savedoff, Levine, and Birdsall (2006); Banerjee and Duflo (2008); and Shadish and Myers (2004).
2. This section draws heavily on a background paper by Grindle (2008) commissioned for this project.

Federal systems: a COD Aid proposal for Mexico's upper secondary schools

The initial impetus for developing the Cash on Delivery Aid (COD Aid) concept was to improve the effectiveness of foreign aid. But it quickly became apparent to us that a similar mechanism could also be useful where central governments make financial transfers to state, provincial, and other subnational levels of government.[1] Just as with the relationship between funders and recipients in the foreign aid context, federal and state governments have some interests in common and others that diverge. Further, the central government lacks information available to state actors about local political interests and implementation capacity. These two features—the divergence of interests and the asymmetry of information—generate a principal-agent problem between the federal and state governments, just as between a funder and recipient in the context of foreign aid.

Wherever a federal government uses fiscal transfers to fund public services in states that exercise a significant degree of autonomy, problems that parallel those of foreign aid are likely. In particular, the paradox that outside aid can undermine local institutional development is a real risk.[2] As with foreign aid, intranational fiscal transfers can soften the budget constraint facing states, permitting excessive and less effective spending decisions. As with foreign aid, fiscal transfers from central governments are sometimes volatile and unpredictable. They can also give state authorities access to privileges and rents that reinforce their power and weaken their accountability to constituents.[3] And they can reduce a state's incentive to mobilize its own tax revenues, reinforcing its reliance on those fiscal transfers.

Depending on the character and quality of federal programs, intranational fiscal transfers may have a variety of other problems in common with foreign aid. While developing country governments must often contend

The overlap of constituencies often generates competition for authority, resources, and recognition

with a large number of bilateral aid agencies, multilateral institutions, and nongovernmental organizations with competing programs, states most often face a single federal government. Even so, to the extent that the federal government has multiple programs across different agencies, the state's administrative burdens and political difficulties in managing this array of programs may be significant. And if the federal government can pay higher salaries, it may, like many foreign aid programs, attract qualified personnel away from state positions.

The essential difference between foreign aid and intranational fiscal transfers is that the state and federal governments are linked by a common political system and overlapping constituencies. While the taxpayers who finance a U.S. aid program for India do not vote in Indian elections, the local beneficiaries of a public service provided in Uttar Pradesh are constituents of both their state and federal governments. Thus, when intranational fiscal transfers occur, officials on both sides of the transfer are accountable to the same constituents through the domestic political system and are likely to be more responsive to those constituents than a foreign aid agency might be.

The overlap of constituencies often generates competition between national and state officials for authority, resources, and recognition. This can improve program effectiveness when the competition is substantive and transparent—when federal officials try one approach, state officials try others, and everyone understands whose programs and whose resources are leading to which outcomes. In this case, constituents can assess the different programs and authorities and reward those who are most effective.

In most instances, however, competition is about claiming credit and is not transparent. Indeed, officials may see it in their interest to confuse the lines of accountability, claiming credit for effective programs and blaming others for ineffective ones. For example, federal officials may be unwilling to fund and design a program for states to implement if they believe the states will take credit for success and blame them for failures. But state officials may be unwilling to accept the responsibility of implementing federal programs unless they can claim credit for successes. As long as federal and state officials focus on claiming credit rather than achieving outcomes, lines of accountability will remain confused to their overlapping constituencies.

COD Aid can address this by increasing the transparency of federal-state relationships. If the federal and state governments agree on a shared goal and make the COD Aid agreement public, roles and responsibilities are much clearer to officials at the two levels of government and to their overlapping constituencies. With federal payment for verified outcomes and state responsibility for progress, the COD Aid agreement clarifies the accountability of each level of government. To the degree that the COD Aid agreement facilitates achieving the shared goal, it also boosts the credibility of both levels of government, as constituents see their tax money used effectively to accomplish public goals.

> The proposal here represents our reflections on how a COD Aid proposal could work in Mexico

The rest of this chapter uses the improvement of upper secondary education in Mexico as an illustration of how COD Aid could work in an intranational fiscal transfer. The idea was presented at a workshop in March 2008 in Mexico City. Workshop participants discussed Mexico's secondary schooling system, current federal government policies and initiatives, and the advantages of applying a COD Aid approach to the relationship between Mexico's federal and state governments. Participants included representatives from the federal and state governments, several Mexican nongovernmental organizations and private philanthropic foundations, international agencies and other experts. The material presented here was derived from the workshop discussions and complemented by additional research. Please note that the proposal discussed here is not endorsed by the government of Mexico. It simply represents our reflections on how a COD Aid proposal could work in Mexico based on the workshop discussions.

Upper secondary education in Mexico: the context

In Mexico, education is divided into primary (*primária*, grades 1–6), secondary (*secundária*, grades 7–9), upper secondary (*média superior*, grades 10–12), and tertiary (*superior*, university level). Primary and secondary school are mandatory for all children. The Mexican education system has expanded substantially over the last few decades, with an enrollment of 9 million children in 1970 rising to more than 20 million in 2000. The population's average years of schooling (for those over 15) has risen from 6.8 years in 1993 to 7.6 in 2003.

Even so, many children repeat school years and drop out of school entirely, and those who graduate frequently have not mastered the skills and knowledge that they should. Based on recent data, 97 percent of Mexican children can be expected to enter primary school, but only 68 percent of the age cohort can expect to graduate from grade 9, and only 35 percent will graduate from upper secondary school.[4] Mexican students regularly score poorly when compared with students in other Latin American countries on international tests, such as the language arts test in the *Laboratorio Latinoamericano* student assessments by the United Nations Educational, Scientific, and Cultural Organizations in 2000.

Since 1993, Mexico's state governments have assumed responsibility for most public upper secondary schools. Of 12,481 upper secondary schools enrolling 3.7 million students, the 31 state governments operate 5,520 (43 percent), the federal government continues to directly operate 1,373 (11 percent), and public universities operate another 624 (5 percent). The remaining 5,117 (41 percent) are private. But the federal government is responsible for setting norms and standards for all

The federal government is introducing new standardized testing, building infrastructure, and experimenting with financial incentives

upper secondary schools, including teacher qualifications, curriculum, and standardized testing.

Upper secondary schools have expanded along with the rest of the education system, but they lose or underserve students at an unacceptable rate. Some 15 percent of students drop out of upper secondary schools each year, and those who graduate are often poorly prepared for college. Observers attribute the relatively poor performance in upper secondary schooling to problems of inadequate teacher training; poor management and supervision of teachers; few incentives for teachers or administrators to innovate; rule-bound thinking by teachers, administrators, and policy-makers; weak parental involvement; weak accountability to citizens; and resistance to change by teacher unions.

Federal responses since 2006

The federal government has initiated programs to address these challenges, introducing new standardized testing, building infrastructure, and experimenting with financial incentives. To monitor student learning, it has been reviewing the upper secondary curriculum and developing standardized tests to assess whether students are mastering it. And to improve accountability to the public, it is making test scores for each school available online.

The federal government is indirectly supporting improvements in the upper secondary schools operated by state governments with funding for infrastructure, scholarships to encourage equity, and internship programs to link school curricula with job-relevant training. To encourage state school systems to experiment with new approaches, it has also set aside money for an Upper Secondary Education Innovation Fund. States can apply for funding under this program for a wide range of initiatives. Once approved, the federal funds are disbursed matching the state's own contribution. Alternatively, up to half the state's contribution can be paid by private philanthropic organizations.

The federal government is also making changes in its own upper secondary schools, hoping to demonstrate effective approaches for the states to adopt. It has changed the way that principals are selected, creating a process of open competitions that emphasize selection based on merit. It is also introducing financial incentives for improvements in student performance—incentives paid to students, teachers, and principals to increase their interest in improved outcomes.

Most federal and state programs are still traditional in the sense that they focus on inputs (infrastructure, teacher training, hiring) and allocate budgets based on historical spending or population rather than outcomes or performance. Even so, many of the initiatives noted above are exceptions to this pattern, such as efforts to introduce financial incentives, merit-based promotions, and competition for funds for innovative state programs. None of the programs, however, focuses attention as strictly on results and with as much autonomy for the recipient as would a COD Aid funding arrangement.

How COD Aid could work for Mexico's upper secondary system

This is a propitious time for trying a COD Aid approach in Mexico's upper secondary schooling system. Recent initiatives are already moving away from a management culture focused on rules to one that emphasizes incentives and outcomes. The Upper Secondary Education Innovation Fund could be the mechanism for implementing a COD Aid initiative. Mexico's strong system of data collection and testing would provide further support for implementing a COD Aid agreement.

Funding mechanism and COD provisions

In 2008, the federal government's budget for improving state-operated upper secondary schools had $77 million (M$830 million) for infrastructure and another $2.8 million (M$30 million) for the Innovation Fund.[5, 6] The federal government could implement changes in the Innovation Fund fairly easily so that all or part of this money would be available to states that have entered an agreement based on COD Aid concepts.

One idea for constructing a COD agreement between Mexico's federal government and its states would rely on existing federal data on the number of students in the third year of upper secondary school and their test scores. The federal government could create an index that would be the product of these two numbers (number of students multiplied by average test score). Test scores could be standardized to range from 0 to 1, and the unit of progress that would trigger a COD payment would be defined as the equivalent of one student reaching the maximum score.[7] While attaching payments to average scores or the share of students passing a standard creates an incentive to exclude poorly performing students, this multiplicative measure of progress gives an incentive to include as many students as possible. Each additional student with a score higher than zero would trigger additional transfers.

To illustrate, consider the state in table 6.1. In year 1, 5 of 10 students finish school, giving the state a 50 percent completion rate in its upper secondary schools. In year 2 of the COD agreement, it retains 3 students—Alejandro, Cristina, and Violeta—who would likely have dropped out without the programs and practices in the COD agreement. The state's completion rate thus rises to 80 percent. But because the three students perform more poorly than their peers, the average test score falls by 50 points. With the payment formula proposed above, this overall performance would still release a reward of M$1.7 million. Continuing with this example, in year 3 the state is unable to improve the completion rate.

Recent initiatives in Mexico are already moving to a management culture that emphasizes incentives and outcomes

TABLE 6.1
Example of payment for student completions and test scores

	Completed?	Final test score
Year 1—Children at the age for completing school		
Juan	Yes	350
Jose	Yes	400
Miguel	Yes	300
Marco	Yes	480
Johanna	Yes	300
Veronica	No	
Anna	No	
Pilar	No	
Jorge	No	
Pedro	No	
Share that completed (%) and average test score	50	366
Total score (share that completed × average test score)		1,830
Year 2—Children at the age for completing school		
Elena	Yes	350
Carlos	Yes	400
Javier	Yes	300
Sara	Yes	480
Isabel	Yes	300
Alejandro	Yes	200
Cristina	Yes	200
Violeta	Yes	210
Yesenia	No	
David	No	
Share that completed (%) and average test score	80	305
Total score (share that completed × average test score)		2,395
Difference from previous year		565
COD payment (difference × M$3,000)		M$1,695,000
Year 3—Children at the age for completing school		
Sofia	Yes	600
Adriana	Yes	400
Daniel	Yes	350
Gabriela	Yes	480
Isidoro	Yes	400
Emilio	Yes	200
Enrique	Yes	300
Guadalupe	Yes	210
Jesus	No	
Raul	No	

TABLE 6.1 (continued)
Example of payment for student completions and test scores

	Completed?	Final test score
Share that completed (%) and average test score	80	368
Total score (share that completed × average test score)		2,940
Difference from previous year		545
COD payment (difference × M$3,000)		M$1,635,000

It does, however, raise the students' average test score from 305 to 368. In this case, the state is rewarded with M$1.6 million.

Each year, states that enter the COD agreement would receive a payment for each unit of progress above the previous year (or a moving average of several earlier years). The funds would be provided on a matching basis. State-supplied money would have to be applied to education programs. The federally supplied money could be used by the state for any purpose outlined in its application to the fund, including noneducational expenditures nonetheless aimed at improving schooling, such as transportation or conditional cash transfers to students or their families. The federal government could either establish a maximum payout or rely on projections of expected demands on the Innovation Fund.

Measuring student completion and performance in upper secondary school
In addition to a mechanism for managing and disbursing funds and a formula for calculating payments, a COD agreement requires information on progress—in this case, the number of students and test scores. The Mexican federal-state relationship permits the federal government to measure student performance directly. As long as the states have confidence that the federal government can measure student performance accurately and will not intentionally misreport results to reduce payments, federal administrative data on student completions and test scores could be a basis for COD transfers.

Over the last decade, Mexico has been improving the quality of its education statistics and its system for testing. The most recent part of this effort is the *Evaluación Nacional del Logro Académico en Centros Escolares* (ENLACE), which measures reading and math comprehension at different grade levels. In its earlier version, ENLACE tested students in grades 3 and 6. In 2008, ENLACE Média Superior was initiated to test students in grade 12. Eventually ENLACE will be applied nationally and become a tool for measuring changes in learning over time—in particular, comparing groups of students in one grade level with those of the next cohort at the same grade level. Data from ENLACE, available annually or biannually, could be used for calculating COD payments.

> Each year, states that enter the COD agreement would receive a payment for each unit of progress

> **The agreement preserves the state's autonomy and discretion in the use of funds**

Mexico has three other advantages that would facilitate a COD approach. First, the federal government has continued opening more information to public scrutiny. Student completion rates and test scores are expected to be available publicly in different forms, including online. Second, civil society organizations have emerged to advocate for better education. Groups like *Mexicanos Primero* could perform a social audit by analyzing government information and making it available in forms understandable to the public, such as state or school report cards.[8] Other groups might work directly at the local level, using the newly available information to participate in policy debates and to hold municipalities or states accountable for their performance. Third, large private philanthropic foundations that are specifically concerned with education have been created in Mexico. They can encourage states to enter a COD agreement by offering to pay for a substantial part of the matching contribution.

Concerns

This proposal for extending and improving upper secondary schooling in Mexico retains the core positive features of the COD Aid approach. Payments are made after outcomes are achieved and based on credible reports that measure the unit of progress. The agreement preserves the state's autonomy and discretion in the use of funds as much as possible. The process and results are transparent, transmitted in easily understandable form to the public and to organizations qualified to analyze and verify the reported information. But even well designed programs raise legitimate concerns and these merit review.

One concern of stakeholders was the effect of regional demographic variation on payments under the COD agreement. If some states face declining cohorts in primary school, their potential gains from a COD program would be much smaller than for states where the size of cohorts in primary school is increasing as fast as or faster than the upper secondary system can expand. It is tempting—but unwise—to introduce modifications to the payment system to compensate these disadvantaged states. Such changes would only undermine the federal government's efforts to use its funds to induce upper secondary school completion regardless of where students live.

Another concern is the effectiveness and credibility of the reporting system for both student completions and test scores. Assuaging this concern requires technical analysis, such as assessing the comparability of the test over time. It may also require a third-party auditor to check the reporting process for quality, consistency, reliability, and accuracy. Such an audit would assess whether administration of the test is effective and determine whether cheating is taking place.

A final concern addresses the use of funds by the states. Since the funds are received after the outcomes are achieved and are not tied to purchasing specific inputs, money could be diverted to improper uses. This concern could be met by the federal government's system for auditing state government accounts to ensure that all funds managed by the state are spent on appropriate goods and services. Or the state could propose a specific set of uses for the funds if and when they are received. The proposal would be similar to that for the Innovation Fund, except that it would not present a fixed budget, since the actual amount of payments received would be contingent on the states' ability to improve upper secondary schooling.

The COD Aid approach is feasible for intranational transfers

Our workshop discussions in Mexico showed that the concepts involved in COD Aid can be applied to transfers between central and local governments because of the numerous parallels to foreign aid. The specific example of improving completion rates and learning in upper secondary schooling in Mexico provided us with an opportunity to test our ideas in a specific context. We assessed whether Mexico's federal government could use its Upper Secondary School Innovation Fund to pay states for progress, using an indicator comprising both completion rates and learning. Having considered and debated the concerns raised, we found the idea of applying COD Aid to this case to be entirely feasible. We recommend that other large federated countries use this example to consider whether a COD Aid approach might work for them.

Notes

1. Subnational entities are highly varied and may be denominated states, provinces, districts, municipalities, and so on. For the remainder of this chapter, we refer to them as states. The same issues can arise between a state and a more local government, and between a local government and a school.

2. Moss, Pettersson, and van de Walle 2006.

3. Knack and Rahman 2004; van de Walle 2001.

4. Santibañez, Vernez, and Razquin 2005.

5. Kate Vyborny developed several of these concepts at the workshop and contributed the main draft for this section.

6. The foreign exchange rate in 2007 was about 10.80 Mexican pesos per U.S. dollar.

7. An alternative option would be to multiply the number of students completing by the improvement in students scores for a given cohort. In other words, the students' test scores would be compared with the scores of the same students on the ENLACE test would be administered to students at the beginning and end of upper secondary school. This option would take longer to begin triggering payments, but would be particularly useful if there were significant demographic change (say, due to migration) affecting the composition of students from year to year.

8. *Mexicanos Primero* already publishes a composite index of effectiveness calculated by state. On school report cards, see EQUIP2 (n.d.-a, n.d.-b).

Beyond primary education: COD Aid for other development goals

Throughout this book we have used primary education to illustrate the possible use of Cash on Delivery Aid (COD Aid). The previous chapter extended the example to look at the potential for a COD Aid program in upper secondary education between different levels of government in one country. This brief chapter explores other examples, considering the possibilities for foreign assistance along the principles of COD Aid in other areas of education and in health, infrastructure, environment, and information. On any issue for which shared goals and measurable progress can be defined, aid can be linked to outcomes. Indeed, funders could offer a menu of COD Aid agreements that recipients could choose from.[1]

For any COD Aid program, the main challenges are to reach agreement on a shared goal, identify an appropriate outcome measure, set a fee per unit of progress, and establish a way to report and verify progress. For each example discussed here, we suggest strategies to meet these and other challenges.

Education

In the education sector, COD Aid could be applied for goals beyond primary completion. In countries where access to primary school is already widespread, quality improvement could be the goal. The initial efforts could focus on introducing testing. Once reliable standardized testing is in place, improvements in average scores would be rewarded directly. Another option would be to reward secondary school completion in much the same way as the primary completion payment proposed above. Or as for Mexico (chapter 6), the reward could be for a combination of enrollment and test scores in the final year of secondary school.

Health

In the health sector, the Global Alliance for Vaccines and Immunisation (GAVI) already operates a program that is in many ways similar to COD Aid (box 7.1). GAVI's Immunization Services Support program works with countries that are eligible because they have low immunization coverage and a plan to expand that coverage. The program provides upfront grants along with a reward of $20 per additional child vaccinated.

COD Aid could also be useful for improving the effectiveness of funds addressing a single disease, such as the U.S. President's Emergency Plan for AIDS Relief

---

BOX 7.1

The Global Alliance for Vaccinations and Immunisation and its audit requirements

The Global Alliance for Vaccines and Immunisation (GAVI) requires that countries pass a data quality audit before receiving reward shares under its Immunization Support Services scheme. The audit assesses the country's capacity to collect accurate data. It then identifies areas needing improvement and assigns a score. GAVI requires that countries pass an audit with a score of 0.80 to receive reward shares, but countries can continue to receive basic funding as they improve their data on immunization coverage.

The audit includes an interview and survey component with officials, and a component similar to an accounting audit. Districts to be audited are chosen randomly, and a team of external and national auditors checks the consistency of the record books of the clinics with regional data. Over the course of the program, several of the countries significantly improved their data collection. The GAVI evaluation notes that reward shares are an incentive that "appears to have had significant impact in motivating countries to address the problem of data quality," an important objective of our COD Aid proposal as well.

While GAVI has achieved many goals, it has also illustrated what occurs when baseline data are overestimated and outcome-oriented programs rely on the implementing agency to report progress. In Kenya, officials decided to use government estimates to establish the baseline of immunization coverage, even though population surveys indicated that coverage rates were lower. With this higher initial baseline, subsequent measures of progress have probably underestimated the true expansion of coverage. Kenya may thus have received fewer reward shares than it might have. The program evaluation recommended establishing an appeals process of some kind to address such situations. A similar proposal is contained in the sample COD Aid contract in the appendix.

A more common problem appears to be overestimating progress. A recent study compared officially reported coverage rates to estimates from other data sources. While the official report indicated 13.9 million additional children had been immunized with diphtheria, tetanus, and pertussis (DTP-3), other sources estimated the number at 5.7–9.2 million children. The study concluded that independent monitoring of health indicators is necessary, especially when foreign assistance is being disbursed against performance. The requirement in a COD Aid agreement that a third party independently verify progress explicitly addresses this concern.

Source: Chee and others 2004; Lim and others 2008.

(PEPFAR). PEPFAR's focus on results is troubling to many AIDS experts because the indicators chosen by the fund are considered to be off the mark. The number of patients receiving treatment, for example, is an inadequate and misleading indicator for the actual goal: reduced morbidity and mortality.[2] Rewards based on other indicators, such as reduced incidence of HIV from a baseline, would provide better incentives for prevention. Better indicators and other improvements following the principles of the COD Aid approach could be incorporated into PEPFAR and other HIV/AIDS programs (box 7.2).

It may also be possible to link funding directly to outcomes for other more general goals in the health sector, such as reducing the disease burden or reducing morbidity or mortality.[3] Again, the outcome indicator is crucial and would require careful background work to ensure accurate measurement, avoid perverse incentives, and reduce

---

BOX 7.2
A COD Aid approach to treating and preventing HIV/AIDS

After 30 years and billions of dollars spent combating AIDS, the rate of new infections remains higher than the rate of placing new patients in treatment. In countries where incidence has declined, it remains difficult to attribute the decline to interventions funded by governments or foreign assistance. The combination of high rates of new infection and increasing numbers of people on lifetime treatment means that even when programs like PEPFAR are successful, they may coexist with a growing number of people living with HIV.

The COD Aid approach could be applied both to treating HIV/AIDS and preventing its spread. For treatment, a COD Aid agreement would reward programs that not only identify newly infected individuals and initiate treatment but also ensure that an individual remains in treatment. A payment formula that successively increases the size of the reward for each year that an individual maintains treatment would be one way to do this.

Applying the COD approach to HIV prevention is more challenging—for at least two reasons. First, a prevention program needs to reach a much larger population. Second, an appropriate unit of progress for such a program is more difficult to design. Change in the prevalence rate (the share of people living with HIV/AIDS) is not a good measure because it is affected both by new infections (which raise the rate) and by deaths (which lower it). Instead, an appropriate indicator might be the rate of new infections over a defined period (such as the annual incidence rate).

But directly measuring the annual incidence rate is challenging. It requires an effective system for selecting a random sample of people from the same cohort and then contacting and testing them annually for HIV infection over several years. Such data collection is feasible at a reasonable cost, especially relative to the substantial funding going to AIDS prevention and treatment in recent years. In addition to providing information to calculate COD Aid payments, this survey information would be extremely useful for identifying specific groups and geographic areas where the epidemic is spreading quickly, for managing the epidemic, and for assessing the effectiveness of different strategies.

Source: Institute of Medicine 2007; Bongaarts and others 2008; Hallet and Over forthcoming.

the lag from government interventions to observed changes in the indicator. As in any COD Aid arrangement, however, the payment would give both funder and recipient a reason to improve outcome data, which are useful for many purposes besides administering aid.

Infrastructure

Expanding and improving infrastructure could also be funded through a COD Aid arrangement. As with other sectors, a key issue would be the design of an appropriate indicator. Most infrastructure projects measure progress in outputs, such as the number of water connections or kilometers of roads, when the true ends of these investments are such outcomes as improved health (from drinking safe water), higher household income in outlying areas, and economic growth (through more reliable and less costly transportation).

The World Bank and several bilateral agencies have financed a large number of infrastructure programs under the Global Partnership on Output-Based Aid, which has done a good job of creating programs that provide payments only after the infrastructural investments are complete and delivered. A water program in Mozambique, for example, pays for water connections only after they have been operating for three months. A program in Ghana to subsidize solar photovoltaic electric systems in rural areas pays the implementing agency only after an independent agent has verified delivery.

The Global Partnership on Output-Based Aid approach could be taken closer to the outcome by creating a COD Aid agreement that pays for potable water consumption from in-house water connections as verified by a household survey. The ease of verifying the presence and quality of physical infrastructure sometimes obscures the fact that maintenance, operation, and use of infrastructure are essential if outputs are to continue providing real benefits.

Environment

The COD Aid concept could also be applied to improving and preserving the environment. For example, it could be used to encourage reductions in carbon emissions. Aid for reducing carbon emissions faces the challenge of identifying and measuring marginal improvement through individual projects. This creates a perverse incentive for countries to allow the design of highly polluting facilities and then seek payments for blocking their completion or upgrading them to greener technology.[4] A COD approach would be compatible with recent proposals for an updated international agreement, which may eventually link funding to the total carbon emissions in a country by paying developing countries per ton of emissions below a baseline or trend.

A program with many similarities to COD Aid has been launched in Brazil. The Amazon Fund was created to raise funds based on measurable reductions of emissions from deforestation in the Amazon (box 7.3). The funding is allocated to projects that combat deforestation and promote conservation.

Access to quality information

The COD Aid approach could also improve the quality of statistics in developing countries. Basic data on population size, health, and education are essential for

---

BOX 7.3
The Amazon Fund

Global warming is accelerating because of both the increased emissions of carbon dioxide and the reduced ability of the earth to absorb carbon dioxide from the environment. The latter results from the vast amounts of deforestation that take place annually. Deforestation in developing countries alone accounts for almost 20 percent of global greenhouse gas emissions, which is equivalent to almost all emissions due to transportation.[1] Three-quarters of the emissions from Brazil, the fourth greatest carbon emitter in the world, are a result of deforestation.[2]

The Brazilian government has taken several measures to curb deforestation. It has drafted and enacted the Action Plan for the Prevention and Control of Deforestation in the Amazon and has set a goal of stopping the loss of forest cover by 2015. The federal government is investing roughly $500 million (for 2008–11) in initiatives to reduce deforestation and promote conservation in the Amazon, but it estimates that it will need an additional $1 billion annually to achieve the goals outlined in the plan.[3]

To raise additional funds to achieve these goals, the government launched the Amazon Fund in 2006. The Amazon Fund is a private fund managed by the Brazilian Development Bank that raises funds based on measurable reductions in deforestation. The data and calculations of deforestation rate reductions and avoided emissions are attested by a scientific board and audited by an international third party. Contributions from official donors, corporations, and individuals in and outside Brazil are allocated to projects that combat deforestation and promote conservation and sustainable use of the Amazon biome. The first contributor to the fund was the Norwegian government, which committed up to $1 billion (for 2008–15) to be disbursed based on verified reductions in deforestation against a 10-year baseline.

While the fund differs from COD Aid in several respects, the role of the Norwegian government and other contributors mirrors the role of funders in a COD Aid program because they commit a certain amount of funding for verified results. The Brazilian Development Bank, by contrast, may incur higher transaction costs than a recipient government that launches a COD Aid program because the bank is required to raise funds every year commensurate with verified progress. In other words, a single set of donors is not required to enter a multiyear commitment.

Despite this and other differences, the Amazon Fund provides a real-world example of linking cash to delivery of an environmental good and demonstrates how a funder can make a substantial contribution to a global problem by providing financial resources and allowing recipient countries to determine how to make progress toward a shared goal.

Notes
1. Commission on Climate and Tropical Forests 2009.
2. Norwegian Office of the Prime Minister 2008.
3. Brazilian Ministry of Environment 2006.

> In sum, the COD Aid approach can be applied to many different development objectives

managing and evaluating public services, yet are generally very low in quality and infrequently updated. International agencies commonly aggregate such data despite the inconsistencies. Foreign funders often bypass national data collection systems altogether, commissioning completely separate surveys such as the Demographic and Health Surveys. These parallel efforts do not directly enhance countries' capacity to gather their own quality data.

A COD Aid approach could give countries an incentive to improve their data by linking payments to this outcome. For example, a COD Aid agreement aimed at improving vital statistics could pay countries for more accurately registering births and deaths. The independent audit would provide information that could be used both to calculate the COD Aid payments and to assess and improve the country's data-collection system. A reliable and accurate vital registration system is not trivial. Vital registration is important for demographic research. It can also have a profound impact on the allocation of government funds to different communities, and it can even affect individuals' voting rights and access to public services.

Increasing transparency and promoting democracy

To support increased transparency and the development of civil society, funders could also make incentive payments to countries for making data—such as budget information, health status, or educational attainments—publicly available. Payments could be linked to the share of people who have accessed public information or who are informed about particular facts, verified through surveys. This would encourage governments to make data available and promote its dissemination. This would probably be more effective than current approaches emphasizing particular inputs (producing brochures or radio advertisements) or specific policy changes (freedom of information legislation).[5]

In sum, the COD Aid approach can be applied to many different development objectives. In each case, the specific nature of the objective or the particular institutional setting will present different challenges. Solutions can come from consulting with experts and applying basic principles to identify appropriate units of progress, payment structures, and verification processes.

Notes

1. Barder and Birdsall (2007). This is similar to the principle of the European Community's MDG Contracts, but they are linked to threshold goals rather than incremental progress, and are linked to outcomes only in small part in order to reduce volatility.

2. Hallet and Over forthcoming.

3. Staff at the Bill and Melinda Gates Foundation are exploring "results-based" approaches for their health sector grants (Kress and Shaw 2008). They discuss grants that would pay for key outputs, such as bednets distributed and births attended, with payments at the

level of individual providers and households as well as at local and higher governments. These outputs are related to, but not the same as, the health status outcomes (reduced malaria prevalence, fewer incidents of infant and maternal trauma) that are the true objective of these programs.

4.   Greiner and Michaelowa 2003; Grubb, Vrolijk, and Brack 1998; Thorne and Lèbre La Rovere 1999.

5.   Hubbard 2007; McIntosh 2006.

References

In analyzing and developing the Cash on Delivery Aid proposal, the Center for Global Development commissioned experts to prepare several background papers and essays on specific topics. Working papers by Owen Barder and Nancy Birdsall (2006) and Marlaine Lockheed (2008) are listed in the references below. Additional papers, essays, workshop summaries, and written comments can be found on CGD's website at www.cgdev.org/section/initiatives/_active/codaid/ papers_and_resources.

Acharya, Arnab, Ana Fuzzo de Lima, and Mick Moore. 2003. "The Proliferators: Transactions Costs and the Value of Aid." Brighton, U.K.: Institute of Development Studies.

Advance Market Commitment Working Group. 2005. *Making Markets for Vaccines: Ideas to Action*. Washington, D.C.: Center for Global Development.

Africa Progress Panel. 2008. *Africa's Development: Promises and Prospects*. Geneva: Africa Progress Panel. [www.africaprogresspanel.org/pdf/2008%20Report.pdf].

Banerjee, Abhijit, Rukmini Banerji, Esther Duflo, Rachel Glennerster, and Stuti Khemani. 2008. "Pitfalls of Participatory Programs: Evidence from a Randomized Evaluation in Education in India." NBER Working Paper 14311. National Bureau of Economics Research, Cambridge, Mass.

Banerjee, Abhijit, and Esther Duflo. 2008. "The Experimental Approach to Development Economics." NBER Working Paper 14467. National Bureau of Economics Research, Cambridge, Mass.

Barder, Owen, and Nancy Birdsall. 2006. "Payments for Progress: A Hands-Off Approach to Foreign Aid." Working Paper 102. Center for Global Development, Washington, D.C.

Benavot, Aaron, and Erin Tanner. 2007. "The Growth of National Learning Assessments in the World, 1995–2006." UNESCO Background Paper for Education for All Global Monitoring Report 2008. 2008/ED/EFA/MRT/PI/16. United Nations Educational, Scientific, and Cultural Organization, Paris.

Birdsall, Nancy. 2007. "Do No Harm: Aid, Weak Institutions and the Missing Middle in Africa." *Development Policy Review* 25(5): 575–98.

———. 2008. "Seven Deadly Sins: Reflections on Donor Failings." In William Easterly, ed., *Reinventing Foreign Aid*. Cambridge, Mass.: MIT Press.

Birdsall, Nancy, Stijn Claessens, and Ishac Diwan. 2003. "Policy Selectivity Foregone: Debt and Donor Behavior in Africa" *World Bank Economic Review* 17(3): 409–35.

Björkman, Martina, and Jakob Svensson. 2007. "Power to the People: Evidence from a Randomized Field Experiment of a Community-based Monitoring Project in Uganda." Centre for Economic Policy Research, London. [www.povertyactionlab.com/papers/bjorkman_svensson.pdf].

Bongaarts, John, Thomas Buettner, Gerhard Heilig, and François Pelletier. 2008. "Has the HIV Epidemic Peaked?" *Population and Development Review* 34(2): 199–224.

Brazilian Ministry of Environment. 2006. "Fundo Amazônia." Brasilia: Ministry of Environment. [www.mma.gov.br/estruturas/sfb/_arquivos/fundo_amazonia_2008_95.pdf].

Bruns, Barbara, Alain Mingat, and Ramahatra Rakotomalala. 2003. *Achieving Universal Primary Education by 2015: A Chance for Every Child*. Washington, D.C.: World Bank.

Cammack, Diana. 2007. "The Logic of African Neopatrimonialism: What Role for Donors?" *Development Policy Review* 25(5): 599–614.

Chang, Ha-Joon. 2005. "Understanding the Relationship between Institutions and Economic Development: Some Key Theoretical Issues." Working Paper 209. United Nations University World Institute for Development Economics Research, Helsinki.

Chee, Grace, Rebecca Fields, Natasha Hsi, and Whitney Schott. 2004. "Evaluation of GAVI Immunization Services Support Funding." Abt Associates: Bethesda, Md. [www.gavialliance.org/resources/Evaluation_of_ISS_Funding_Aug04.pdf].

Christian Aid. 2001. "Ignoring the Experts: Poor People's Exclusion from Poverty Reduction Strategies." Policy Briefing. Christian Aid, London. [http://training.itcilo.it/decentwork/staffconf2002/presentations/ref-christianaid-excluding%20the%20poor%20from%20PRSP.pdf].

———. 2002. "Participation in Dialogue? The *Estrategia Boliviana de Reducción de la Pobreza*." Policy Briefing. Christian Aid, London.

Commission for Africa. 2005. *Our Common Interest: Report of the Commission for Africa*. London: Commission for Africa. [http://allafrica.com/sustainable/resources/view/00010595.pdf].

Committee for the Evaluation of the President's Emergency Plan for AIDS Relief (PEPFAR) Implementation. 2007. *PEPFAR Implementation: Progress and Promise*. Edited by Jaime Sepúlveda, Charles Carpenter, James Curran, William Holzemer, Helen Smits, Kimberly Scott, and Michele Orza. Washington, D.C.: National Academies Press.

Commission on Climate and Tropical Forests. 2009. *Protecting the Climate Forests: Why Reducing Tropical Deforestation is in America's Vital National Interest*. Washington, D.C.: Commission on Climate and Tropical Forests. [www.climateforestscommission.org/documents/cctf-report.pdf].

Crouch, Luis, and Jonathan Mitchell. 2008. "Audit Options to Certify Results for a 'Cash on Delivery' Contract in the Education Sector." Center for Global Development, Washington, D.C. [www.cgdev.org/doc/progressbasedaid/CrouchMitchell.pdf].

de Renzio, Paolo, and Warren Krafchik. 2007. "Lessons from the Field: The Impact of Civil Society Budget Analysis and Advocacy in Six Countries." International Budget Project, Washington, D.C. [www.internationalbudget.org/PractitionersGuide.pdf].

Devarajan, Shantayanan, David Dollar, and Torgny Holmgren. 2001. *Aid and Reform in Africa: Lessons from Ten Case Studies*. Washington, D.C.: World Bank.

Development Assistance Committee. 2008a. "Monitoring Resource Flows To Fragile States: 2007 Report." Development Assistance Committee, Paris. [www.oecd.org/dataoecd/4/21/41680220.pdf].

Development Assistance Committee. 2008b. *2008 Survey on Monitoring the Paris Declaration: Making Aid More Effective By 2010.* Paris: Development Assistance Committee. [www.oecd.org/dataoecd/58/41/41202121.pdf].

DFID (U.K. Department for International Development), U.K. Foreign and Commonwealth Office, and Her Majesty's Treasury. 2004. "Partnerships for Poverty Reduction: Changing Aid 'Conditionality'." Department for International Development, London. [www.dfid.gov.uk/Pubs/files/conditionalitychange.pdf].

Easterly, William. 2002. "What Did Structural Adjustment Adjust? The Association of Policies and Growth with Repeated IMF and World Bank Adjustment Loans." Working Paper 11. Center for Global Development, Washington, D.C.

———. 2006. *The White Man's Burden: Why The West's Efforts to Aid the Rest Have Done So Much Ill and So Little Good.* New York: Penguin.

EQUIP2 (Educational Quality Improvement Program). n.d.-a. "Report Cards and Accountability in Decentralized Education Systems." Policy brief. U.S. Agency for International Development, Washington, D.C. [www.equip123.net/docs/e2-ReportCards_PolicyBrief.pdf].

———. n.d.-b. "School Report Cards: Some Recent Experiences." Working paper. U.S. Agency for International Development, Washington, D.C. [www.equip123.net/docs/e2-ReportCards_WP.pdf].

Eichler, Rena, Ruth Levine, and the Performance-Based Incentives Working Group. 2009. *Performance Incentives for Global Health: Potential and Pitfalls.* Washington, D.C.: Center for Global Development.

Eifert, Benn, and Alan Gelb. 2005. "Coping with Aid Volatility." *Finance and Development* 42(3).

European Commission. 2005. "EC Budget Support: An Innovative Approach to Conditionality." European Commission, Brussels. [http://spa.synisys.com/resources/2005/EC_GBS_VT_Review.pdf].

Fritz, Verena, and Alina Rocha Menocal. 2007. "Developmental States in the New Millennium: Concepts and Challenges for a New Aid Agenda." *Development Policy Review* 25(5): 531–52.

Greiner, Sandra, and Axel Michaelowa. 2003. "Defining Investment Additionality for CDM Projects–Practical Approaches." *Energy Policy* 31(10): 1007–15.

Grindle, Merilee. 2007. "Good Enough Governance Revisited." *Development Policy Review* 25(5): 533–74.

———. 2008. "Learning from Cash on Delivery: Research to Accompany a Pilot." Background note. Center for Global Development, Washington, D.C. [www.cgdev.org/doc/Cash%20on%20Delivery%20AID/Grindle%20COD%20research.pdf].

Grubb, M., C. Vrolijk, and D. Brack. 1998. *The Kyoto Protocol: A Guide and Assessment*. London: The Royal Institute of International Affairs/Earthscan.

Hallet, Timothy B., and Mead Over. Forthcoming. "How to Pay Cash on Delivery for HIV Infections Averted: Two Measurement Approaches and Ten Payout Functions." Working paper. Center for Global Development, Washington, D.C.

Harding, April. 2009. *Partnerships with the Private Sector in Health: What the International Community Can Do to Strengthen Health Systems in Developing Countries*. Washington, D.C.: Center for Global Development.

Hausmann, Ricardo, and Dani Rodrik. 2002. "Economic Development as Self-Discovery." NBER Working Paper 8952. National Bureau of Economic Research, Cambridge, Mass.

Herrling, Sheila, and Sarah Rose. 2007. "Will the Millennium Challenge Account Be Caught in the Crosshairs? A Critical Year for Full Funding." Center for Global Development, Washington, D.C. [www.cgdev.org/content/publications/detail/13398].

High Level Forum on Aid Effectiveness. 2005. "Paris Declaration on Aid Effectiveness." Accra.

High Level Forum on Aid Effectiveness, 2008. "Accra Agenda for Action." Accra.

Holland, P.W., and D.B. Rubin, eds. 1982. *Test Equating*. New York: Academic Press.

Hsi, Natasha, and Rebecca Fields. 2004. "Evaluation of GAVI Immunization Services Support Funding Case Study: Kenya" Abt Associates: Bethesda, Md. [www.changeproject.org/pubs/GAVI_Kenya_final.pdf].

Hubbard, Paul. 2007. "Putting the Power of Transparency in Context: Information's Role in Reducing Corruption in Uganda's Education Sector." Working Paper 136. Center for Global Development, Washington, D.C.

IFFIm (International Finance Facility for Immunisation). 2008. "IFFIm: The International Finance Facility for Immunisation." IFFIm Company, London.

International Development Department and Associates. 2006. "Evaluation of General Budget Support: Synthesis Report." Joint Evaluation of Budget Support 1994–2004. University of Birmingham, International Development Department, Birmingham, U.K.

Institute of Medicine. 2007. "PEPFAR Implementation: Progress and Promise." IOM Consensus Report, March 30. Institute of Medicine, Washington, D.C. [www.iom.edu/Reports/2007/PEPFAR-Implementation-Progress-and-Promise.aspx].

Kharas, Homi. 2008. "Measuring the Cost of Aid Volatility." Wolfensohn Center for Development Working Paper 3. Brookings Institution, Washington, D.C.

Killick, Tony, 1998. *Aid and the Political Economy of Policy Change*. London: Routledge.

Knack, Stephen. 2000. "Aid Dependence and the Quality of Governance." Policy Research Working Paper 2396. World Bank, Washington, D.C.

Knack, Stephen, and Aminur Rahman. 2004. "Donor Fragmentation and Bureaucratic Quality in Aid Recipients." Policy Research Working Paper 3186. World Bank, Washington, D.C.

Kress, Dan, and R. Paul Shaw. 2008. "A New Aid Paradigm for Donor Assistance in Health? The Appeal of Results Based Financing." Bill and Melinda Gates Foundation, Seattle, Wash.

Levine, Ruth, Nancy Birdsall, and Amina Ibrahim. 2003. "Achieving Universal Primary Education by 2015." Background paper for the Millennium Project Task Force on Gender Equality and Education." Center for Global Development, Washington, D.C.

Lim, Stephen S., David B. Stein, Alexandra Charrow, and Christopher J.L. Murray. 2008. "Tracking Progress Towards Universal Childhood Immunisation and the Impact of Global Initiatives: A Systematic Analysis of Three-Dose Diphtheria, Tetanus, and Pertussis Immunisation Coverage." *The Lancet* 372(9655): 2031–46.

Linn, Robert. 2005. "Adjusting for Differences in Tests." Paper prepared for a Symposium on the Use of School-Level Data for Evaluating Federal Education Programs, National Academies, Board on Testing and Assessment, December 9, Washington, D.C.

Lockheed, Marlaine. 2008. "Measuring Progress with Tests of Learning: Pros and Cons for 'Cash on Delivery' Aid for Education." Working Paper 147. Center for Global Development, Washington, D.C.

Masters, William A., and Benoit Delbecq. 2008. "Accelerating Innovation with Prize Rewards: History and Typology of Technology Prizes and a New Contest Design for Innovation in African Agriculture." Discussion Paper 835. International Food Policy Research Institute, Washington, D.C.

McIntosh, Toby. 2006. "Freedom of Information Laws Added to the Development Agenda." March 22. [www.freedominfo.org/features/20060322.htm].

Mexicanos Primero Visión 2030 and Fundación IDEA. 2008. *Indice Compuesto de Eficacia de los sistemas escolares*. Mexico City.

Milgrom, Paul, and John Roberts. 1992. *Economics, Organization and Management*. London: Prentice-Hall.

Morley, Samuel, and David Coady. 2003. "From Social Assistance to Social Development: Targeted Education Subsidies in Developing Countries." Center for Global Development, Washington, D.C.

Moss, Todd, Gunilla Pettersson, and Nicolas van de Walle. 2006. "An Aid Institutions Paradox? A Review Essay on Aid Dependency and State Building in Sub-Saharan Africa." Working Paper 74. Center for Global Development, Washington, D.C.

Norwegian Office of the Prime Minister. 2008. "Facts about the Rain Forest and the Amazon Fund." Office of the Prime Minister, Oslo. [www.regjeringen.no/en/dep/smk/Whats-new/news/2008/facts-about-the-rain-forest-and-the-amaz.html?id=526497].

OECD (Organisation for Economic Co-operation and Development). Various years. OECD Stat Extracts: DAC2a ODA Disbursements Table. Paris. [http://stats.oecd.org/WBOS/Index.aspx?DatasetCode=TABLE2A].

———. 2006. "DAC Guidelines and Reference Series Applying Strategic Environmental Assessment: Good Practice Guidance for Development Cooperation." Organisation for Economic Co-operation and Development, Paris.

PEFA (Public Expenditure and Financial Accountability). 2005. "Public Financial Management: Performance Measurement Framework." PEFA Secretariat, Washington, D.C.

Government of Mexico. n.d. Portal ENLACE. [www.enlace.sep.gob.mx]

Pritchett, L. 2002. "It Pays to Be Ignorant: A Simple Political Economy of Rigorous Program Evaluation." *Journal of Policy Reform* 5 (4): 251–69.

Rajan, Raghuran, and Arvind Subramanian. 2005. "What Undermines Aid's Impact on Growth?" International Monetary Fund, Washington, D.C.

Rajani, Rakesh, ed. 2005. *Access to Information in Tanzania: Still A Challenge.* Dar Es Salaam: HakiElimu, Legal Human Rights Centre, and Research on Poverty Alleviation. [www.hakielimu.org/hakielimu/documents/document87report_access_info_tz_challenge_en.pdf].

Randall, Vicky. 2007. "Political Parties and Developmental States." *Development Policy Review* 25(5): 633–52.

Ranis, Gustav. 2008. "The Foreign Aid Paradox—And Opportunity." Center for Global Development, Washington, D.C.

Ravindra, Adikeshavalu. 2004. "An Assessment of the Impact of Bangalore Citizen Report Cards on the Performance of Public Agencies." Evaluation Capacity Development Working Paper 12. World Bank, Operations Evaluation Department, Washington, D.C. [www.gsdrc.org/go/display&type=Document&id=1171].

Rodrik, Dani. 2007. *One Economics, Many Recipes.* Princeton, N.J.: Princeton University Press.

Santibanez, Lucrecia, Georges Vernez, and Paula Razquin. 2005. "Education in Mexico: Challenges and Opportunities." Rand Corporation, Santa Monica, Calif.

Savedoff, William D., Ruth Levine, and Nancy Birdsall. 2006. *When Will We Ever Learn? Improving Lives through Impact Evaluation.* Report of the Evaluation Gap Working Group. Center for Global Development, Washington, D.C.

Selowsky, Marcelo. 2003. "The Role of Fiscal Adjustment in IMF-Supported Programs." International Monetary Fund, Independent Evaluation Office, Washington, D.C.

Shadish, William, and David Myers. 2004. "Campbell Collaboration: Research Design Policy Brief." Campbell Collaboration, Oslo.

Siba, Eyerusalem G. 2008. "Determinants of Institutional Quality in Sub-Saharan African Countries." Gothenburg University, Sweden. [http://gupea.ub.gu.se/dspace/bitstream/2077/10382/1/gunwpe0310.pdf].

Thorne, Steve, and Emilio Lèbre La Rovere. 1999. "Criteria and Indicators for Appraising Clean Development Mechanism (CDM) Projects." Helio Internacional, Paris. [www.pelangi.or.id/database/Artikel/CriteriaPaper.doc].

van de Walle, Nicolas. 2001. *African Economies and the Politics of Permanent Crisis, 1979-1999.* Cambridge, U.K.: Cambridge University Press.

World Bank. 2004. "The Poverty Reduction Strategy Initiative: An Independent Evaluation of the World Bank's Support Through 2003." World Bank, Operations Evaluation Department (now Independent Evaluation Group), Washington, D.C. [http://lnweb90.worldbank.org/oed/oeddoclib.nsf/24cc3bb1f94ae11c85256808006a0046/6b5669f816a60aaf85256ec1006346ac/$FILE/PRSP_Evaluation.pdf].

———. 2008. *World Development Indicators 2008.* Washington, D.C.: World Bank.

———. n.d. "Core Guidance: Preparing Public Expenditure Reviews for Human Development." World Bank, Washington, D.C. [http://siteresources.worldbank.org/EXTPERGUIDE/Resources/PER-Complete.pdf].

Term sheets for COD Aid contracts

This appendix provides term sheets and schedules for two contracts necessary to implement a Cash on Delivery Aid (COD Aid) agreement on primary education. The first contract and schedule detail the relationship and commitments between funders and recipients, and the second those between funders and a "verification agent"—that is, the organization contracted to verify delivery of the outcomes detailed in the first contract. The terms sheets for the contract are generic and can be used for any COD Aid agreement by replacing the education goal with an alternative. In such a case, the schedules presented here—specific to the primary education proposal—would be replaced with correspondingly detailed schedules specific to the alternative goal.

We developed these terms sheets through research and consultation with representatives from government, nongovernmental organizations, research centers, and development agencies. They represent our best effort to propose a set of contracts with a strong likelihood of success, since they address a range of concerns that experts and practitioners raised. Funders and recipients can use this template to draw up contracts that suit their needs. Brackets are used to indicate items that require specification (for example, the baseline of enrollment or the name of an organization). In cases where several options exist and the optimal choice is unclear, we have provided notes that discuss other options.

Model term sheet for Contract 1:

COD Aid agreement between Funder(s) and Recipient(s)

1. Parties: One or more governmental grant-making agencies, multilateral agencies or initiatives, or non-governmental organizations or foundations (each a "**Funder**")[1], and one or more governments or governmental agencies (each an "**Implementing Authority**").[2]

2. Purpose of Contract: Create a legally binding series of agreements that guarantees the Funder(s) will make a fixed payment to the Implementing Authority for each additional unit of progress toward one or more educational goals (the "**Education Goal**"[3]) as specified in Schedule A, "Contract provisions regarding units of measurement and payment."[4]

3. Benefits to Funder: Fulfills the Funder's philanthropic mission (in the case of a non-governmental entity) and/or the Funder's statutory or regulatory mandate (in the case of a governmental entity) by (a) giving the Implementing Authority(s) an incentive to accelerate progress in reaching the Education Goal, (b) providing the Implementing Authority(s) with financial resources that can be used flexibly to advance the Education Goal, and (c) reducing the administrative burden of providing financial assistance to reach the Education Goal.

4. Benefits to Implementing Authority: Allows the Implementing Authority (a) to pursue a comprehensive strategy for reaching the Education Goal with less intrusive engagement by the Funder(s); (b) to use the Funder(s)' financial assistance in whatever manner it chooses to reach the Education Goal most effectively and efficiently; (c) to reduce the administrative burden of receiving financial assistance; (d) to shift accountability for the use of financial assistance from foreign taxpayers to domestic constituencies; and (e) to reorient the discussion between the Funder(s) and the Implementing Authority(s) from a focus on inputs to a focus on measurement and results.

5. Conditions of payment: Funder(s) agree(s) to pay the Implementing Authority an amount for each unit of progress as specified in Schedule A, with no minimum targets to activate payment and no restrictions on the use of the funds.

6. Term: The contract term is five years, with the expectation that it will be renewed in five-year increments.

7. Reporting: The Implementing Authority will submit annual reports on progress toward the Education Goal within the time-frame set forth in Schedule A.

8. Verification: The Funder(s) will contract a firm or agency from the list in Schedule B (hereafter the **Verification Agent**[5]) to audit the government's report and verify its accuracy through the use of independently collected information (for example, a

[1] Funders can be bilateral and multilateral agencies, private foundations, or other non-governmental actors.

[2] This is written with national governments in mind. But the Implementing Authority could be a ministry of education, ministerial department (for example, for primary education), subnational government, or non-governmental or private education system.

[3] See chapter 3 for a detailed discussion on choosing the education goal.

[4] The contract could be aimed at goals in other sectors instead.

[5] The Verification Agent can be a consulting firm, research firm, or agency selected by the Funder(s) from a list of agents agreed to by the Funder(s) and the Implementing

statistically representative survey). The Implementing Authority will allow the Verification Agent the access needed to complete this report.

9. Additionality: The Funder(s) commits to ensuring that the payments made under this contract are treated as additional to other assistance provided in or to the country of the Implementing Authority. The Funder(s) commits to abide by existing aid commitments and to act in good faith so that the payments made under this contract are treated as additional to other forms of financial assistance by the Funder(s).

10. Termination and indemnification: The Implementing Authority can terminate the contract at any time upon giving 90 days notice. In such an event, the Implementing Authority will forfeit any payments associated with progress subsequent to the previous annual progress report and can make no further claims on the Funder with respect to this contract. The Funder can terminate the contract with 90 days notice after paying a penalty equivalent to the expected value of the contract to the Implementing Authority over the remaining term of the contract, as determined by an independent committee (hereafter the **Arbitration Committee**) to be selected according to procedures detailed in Schedule C.[6]

11. Dispute resolution: The Funder and Implementing Authority may appeal any unresolved disputes to an Arbitration Committee, comprised of five individuals mutually agreed upon by the Parties according to procedures detailed in Schedule C. Members of the Arbitration Committee will be reimbursed for reasonable travel expenses and paid a reasonable honorarium in compensation for their service. The plaintiff will pay the expenses of the Arbitration Committee; however, plaintiff can be reimbursed for these expenses if the appeal is successful, at the discretion of the Committee.

12. Public disclosure: The contents of this contract, the reports on progress with respect to the Education Goal, and the report of the Verification Agent will be publicly disseminated as set forth in Schedule A.

13. Accompanying research: The Implementing Authority is obligated to allow and facilitate research into how education policies and institutions may change as a result of this contract. Although the Implementing Authority has no obligation to finance such research, it is required to facilitate researchers' access to primary educational and public finance data, including test scores at the individual level with appropriate safeguards to ensure privacy of the individuals who have been tested. The final research report will be subject to external peer review before publication, and appropriate measures will be taken to protect privacy of all individuals.

14. Dispute resolution: [TBD]

Authority(s) as part of this contract (see Schedule A). This list could be established by requesting initial bids from interested organizations, which could be reviewed and approved by the Funder(s) and Implementing Authority before finalizing the contract. Schedule B would be a list, and a model version is not included in this appendix.

[6] A model for Schedule C is not included in this appendix. It would provide procedures and criteria for selecting an Arbitration Committee in the event of a dispute between the parties. It could establish a process for each party to nominate individuals for the committee. The criteria would require that individuals serving on the Arbitration Committee are internationally respected individuals who are not citizens of the countries involved in the dispute and who have relevant expertise in law, education, finance, or the social sciences.

15. Governing law: [TBD]

16. Waiver of immunity: [Appropriate provisions to ensure that if either or both parties are sovereign, they will be bound by the terms of the contract]

17. Force majeure: [TBD]

18. Other provisions: [TBD]

Model term sheet for Contract 1, Schedule A:

Specification of the Education Goal for the COD Aid agreement between Funder(s) and Recipient(s)

1. Education Goal: The Education Goal is to ensure that every child completes a good quality primary education.[1]

2. Units of measurement and payment: The Funder commits to pay the Implementing Authority $20 per assessed completer to a maximum set by the Base Year Enrollment of [NUMBER] students[2] and $200 per assessed completer in excess of the Base Year Enrollment.[3] Upon first renewing the contract (after 5 years), the Base Year Enrollment will be adjusted annually, becoming equal to the total number of assessed completers five years earlier.

3. Assessed completers: An assessed completer is a student who is enrolled in the terminal year of primary school and who takes an approved standardized test. The examination must be a standardized test of relevant competencies that is equated to permit comparisons from year to year and which is mutually accepted by the Funder and the Implementing Authority.[4]

4. Reporting: The Implementing Authority will report the number of assessed completers and average test scores for each primary school to the Funder and the Verification Agent in a timely fashion. The information will be provided in a format that facilitates analysis of the information's validity, reliability, accuracy, and ease of dissemination.

5. Verification: The Verification Agent will conduct a retest of a random sample of schools within 3 weeks of the official test. The date of the retest will be public information but the exact schools chosen will be known only to the Verification Agent. The sample will be large enough to test, with 95 percent confidence, that the official report is no more than 5 percent above the Verification Agent's estimate of the true number of assessed completers. The Verification Agent will also gather information from schools regarding enrollment to compare with the list of eligible assessed completers and compare test scores to identify significant discrepancies that might indicate manipulation of results.

[1] Other education goals that have been suggested include improved quality of schooling, numbers of students completing primary school, and numbers of students successfully entering or completing secondary school. For further discussion, see chapter 3.

[2] The base year enrollment may not be known with certainty if the Implementing Authority's education information system is unreliable. What is essential is that the two parties agree on a number for the base year enrollment, specified here, to determine the level at which the higher payment is triggered.

[3] For a discussion on setting the amount of the payment, see chapter 3.

[4] The specific exam does not have to be agreed upon before the contract is signed. The criteria for an acceptable exam and a process for judging whether the test meets those criteria are required before signature. See chapter 3 for a detailed discussion of testing and criteria.

6. Conditions for and timing of payments: The Funder will make payments as specified in Contract 1, Schedule A, Item 2 after: (a) the Verification Agent's Report confirms that the Implementing Authority's reported number of assessed completers is no more than 5 percent higher than the estimated number of assessed completers; (b) the Implementing Authority is complying with the commitment to publicly disseminate the number of assessed completers and test scores at the school level; and (c) the Implementing Authority is cooperating with researchers who have been contracted to evaluate the COD Aid agreement. This payment will be effected within three (3) months of receiving the Implementing Authority's Report. [5]

7. Discrepancies between official and estimated test results: If the Verification Agent finds that the Implementing Authority's Report overstates the number of assessed completers by more than 5 percent (with 95 percent statistical confidence), then the amount paid by the Funder will be reduced and calculated as follows. The Verification Agent's estimate of total assessed completers (V1) will be divided by the Implementing Authority's reported number of assessed completers (I1) to calculate a Quotient (Q). The amount paid for each assessed completer up to the Base Year Enrollment (as described in Item 2) will be equal to the Quotient (Q) multiplied by $20, and the amount paid for each assessed completer in excess of Base Year Enrollment (as described in Item 2) will be the Quotient (Q) multiplied by $200.

8. Public dissemination: The Implementing Authority will publicly disseminate its report on assessed completers and average test scores for each school, and by gender and ethnic or racial classifications reported in the most recent census.[6]

9. Eligibility: The Implementing Authority will be eligible only if it (a) operates in a low-income country (as defined by the World Bank); and (b) is legally responsible for providing primary education to a large share of the population in a relevant geographic area.[7][8]

[5] The level of disaggregation in the publicly disseminated report could be set at the school, school district, municipal, or state levels. It should be set at the finest level of disaggregation that is possible relative to the precision and reliability of the information.

Initially, national test scores could be reported publicly, with the level of disaggregation increasing over time as confidence in the national learning assessment's validity and reliability increase.

[6] See note [5].

[7] Alternative eligibility criteria could be used. For example, middle-income countries could be included, with the expectation that the amount of money would be most attractive to lower income countries.

[8] Additional eligibility could be included to address such factors as reliable information systems, good quality data collection, institutional capacity, availability of standardized tests, effective governance in managing public funds, and participation in an international sector strategy process (for example, SWAPs or FTI). But adding such restrictions would preclude COD Aid agreements with many countries that might otherwise benefit significantly (see chapter 2).

Model term sheet for Contract 2:
Contract between Funder(s) and Verification Agent

1. Parties: The **Funder**(s) party to Contract 1 and a consulting firm, research firm, or agency (hereafter the **Verification Agent**) selected through the process specified in Contract 1.

2. Purpose of contract: To create a legally binding agreement by which the Funder(s) appoints the Verification Agent to verify the accuracy of each annual Report on Progress provided by the Implementing Authority (as specified in Contract 1, Schedule A, Item 6).

3. Term: The term of this contract shall be the same as the initial term of Contract 1.

4. Report: The Verification Agent shall submit its Verification Report to the Funder(s) and Implementing Authority within 4 weeks of completing a retest of sample schools.

5. Compensation: Funder(s) agree(s) to pay Verification Agent annually [cost plus fee] upon determining that the annual Verification Report meets the standards set forth in Contract 2, Schedule A. If the Funder(s) does not make such a determination within 30 days of receiving the report, the Funder(s) is obligated to pay the annual fee in full.

6. Termination: If Contract 1 for any reason is terminated or otherwise becomes void, Verification Agent shall cease work on the current Verification Report. Verification Agent shall then present an invoice and Funder(s) shall compensate Verification Agent for expenditures made on the current Verification Report.

7. Dispute resolution: [Process for resolution of disputes between Funder and Verification Agent or Implementing Authority and Verification Agent.]

Model term sheet for Contract 2, Schedule A:
Specification of the Verification Report in the case of Primary Education

1. Purpose: The Verification Report will provide adequate information to judge the accuracy of the annual Report on Progress submitted by the Implementing Authority. The Report on Progress will be considered accurate if the Verification Agent can demonstrate with 95 percent confidence that the number of assessed completers in the Report on Progress is no more than 5 percent greater than the Verification Agent's estimate of the true number of assessed completers.

2. Content: The Verification Report will verify the quality of the data presented in the Report on Progress by the Implementing Authority.

3. Transparency: The Verification Report will include a full description of the methods, sampling, data collection, data, analysis, and conclusions.

4. Characteristics of Data Quality Verification: the Verification Agent will review and assess the data, reporting, and procedures used by the Implementing Authority to prepare its Report on Progress. This review will include normal audit procedures and the results of a retest of a randomly selected nationally representative sample of schools.

The Verification Agent will verify the reported numbers of students taking the approved test and the number of assessed completers according to agreed parameters (for example, enrollment in final year of primary school) as specified in Contract 1, Schedule A.

The Verification Agent will verify the reported average test scores for each school and for the nationally representative sample as specified in Contract 1, Schedule A.

The Verification Agent will verify that the test is comparable from one year to the next and that it meets previously agreed upon standards as set forth in Contract 1, Schedule A.

Index

A

accountability

among funders, recipients, and constituents, 21–22

as a challenge of foreign aid, 8–9

accuracy, defining for audit results, 61

Action Plan for the Prevention and Control of Deforestation in the Amazon, 101

additionality, 68–69

adjustment loans, waiving conditions on, 14

administration, aid programs competing for people skilled in, 4

administrative costs

of aid to recipients in Vietnam, 5

entailed by audit, 61

reduced by an open contract, 71

adverse events, financing and, 71

agents, pool of mutually acceptable, 73

agreement, for primary education, 45–46

aid. *See* foreign aid

Amazon Fund, in Brazil, 100–101

ambiguity, less with COD Aid, 22

analysis, research strategies at two levels of, 78

arbitration

process for, 63

required for COD Aid agreements, 73

arbitration committee, 73, 113

assessed completers

assigning a unique identification number, 60

calculating number of additional, 53

COD Aid contract outline, 47

consequences of overstating, 62

defined, 114

determining additional, 53

disclosure of, 59

drawing attention to content and quality of schooling, 49

encouraging development of management information and testing systems, 50–51

independent audit of number of, 59–62

measuring progress by number of, 48–53

number

of additional, 55

of easily defined, 48–49

relatively easy to audit, 49–50

as unit of progress, 46

assessments

COD Aid fostering, 25

standards-based, 50

asymmetric information, effect on local production function, 9

attendance, maximizing for a retest, 60

attribution, confirming in research, 81

auditing, number of assessed completers, 49–50

auditors, preapproved list of mutually acceptable, 20

audits, role of independent, 59–62

average test scores. *See also* test(s)

consequences of overstating, 62

disclosure of, 59

sample size necessary to estimate, 61

B

Bangalore, India, citizen report card, 58

baseline

for calculating payment, 55

establishing for process approach, 82

of students completing primary school, 53

baseline data, overestimating, 98

bilateral agencies, offering COD Aid, 72

Bill and Melinda Gates Foundation, 70

binding constraints, recipients addressing, 24

borrower-recipient, in a COD Aid agreement, 69

Brazil, emissions as a result of deforestation, 101
Brazilian Development Bank, 101
budget support
    loans, 11
    multiple performance and progress measures of, 38
    reducing administrative burden on recipient governments, 7
    requiring substantial ongoing funder scrutiny, 7
    support programs, 37–38
budgets, allocating, 90
buy-downs, trust fund established for, 70

C

carbon emissions, aid for reducing, 100
Cash on Delivery Aid. *See* COD (Cash on Delivery) Aid
cash transfer programs, conditional, 37
causation, confirming in research on a COD Aid agreement, 81
central governments, making financial transfers to other levels of government, 87
cheating, on test performance increasing the cost of auditing, 52
child support grants, disparities and declines in South Africa, 58
citizen report card, in Bangalore, India, 58
civil society organizations, emerging to advocate for better education, 94
COD (Cash on Delivery) Aid
    advantages of, 21–30
    affecting funder and recipient behaviors, 76
    agreements
        analysis of validity of, 83
        challenges of implementing and financing, 74
        choosing a simple incentive, 64
        clarifying accountability of each level of government, 88
        contingency provisions, 62–63
        in the education sector, 46, 47
        between funders and recipients, 112–114
        funding, 67–71
        implementation of, 71–74
        influence of various actors on, 80
        institutions and initiatives to support or administer, 72
        issues regarding funding and implementing, 67–74
        keeping simple, 63–65
        on primary education, 111
        requiring arbitration, 73

    requiring information on progress, 93

    role of third parties in, 73–74

    specification of education goals, 114–115

    supporting other ways of verifying progress, 65

    transparent reporting and verification, 55, 58–62

    using existing expertise to develop, 65

    ways to implement, 72

applications of, 17

basics of, 18

benefits of, 26

building on other results-based aid programs, 36–38

changing roles of funders and recipients, 23

characteristics of, 39

compared to budget support, 38

complementary to other aid programs, 18, 19

complementing budget support, 29, 38

concerns and risks, 30–35

contract elements, 45

contracts

    described, 17

    elements for COD Aid, 20

    less ambiguous for COD Aid, 21–22

    levels of disclosure, 59

    outline to pay for assessed completers, 47

    public nature and transparency of, 55

    raising matching private money or borrowing against, 31–32

    term sheets and schedules for, 111–117

coordinating actions of official funders, 27–28

core of, 17

displacing other aid programs, 30, 68

effectiveness, 27–30, 76

as extreme innovation, 75

as feasible, 63, 95

foreign assistance along principles of, 97

fostering accountability, 21–22

GAVI compared to, 36

as a global compact, 28

initiative, research accompanying, 76–79

as an intranational fiscal transfer, 89

introducing change, 26

judging based on strengths and weaknesses, 69

key features, 18–20, 45

meetings and events with discussions of, 12, 13

as more predictable, 38

moving to, 39

as needed in foreign aid, 39

operating at macro level, 37

as part of an existing multilateral initiative, 72

as a possible approach to reform, 13–14

programs, main challenges for, 97

risks, 30–35

solutions to bureaucratic rigidities, 68

steps, 20

success of, 40, 78

as too little, too late, 31

unintended consequences of, 32

using for transfers between a variety of actors, 17

waste and corruption and, 33–34

comparative case approach, to research on COD Aid agreement, 83

comparative work, entailing isolating relevant policy reform initiatives, 82

comparators, as similar to and different from COD Aid agreement, 82

competition, generated by overlapping constituencies, 88

completion with a five-year lag, as the baseline, 53

conditionality

introduction to, 6

policy-based loans with, 11

consequences, of COD Aid, 32

constituencies, overlap of generating competition, 88

contingencies, provision for in COD Aid agreement, 62–63

contracts. *See* COD (Cash on Delivery) Aid, contracts

corruption, COD Aid encouraging, 33–34

cost-reimbursement contract, 10, 11

costs. *See also* administrative costs

of arbitration procedure, 73

of audits, 61

paying for test development and implementation, 52

counterfactuals, establishing in impact evaluation design, 77

countries

encouraging self-selection by, 71

policies, vetting of, 72

receiving more than 10 percent of GDP in aid, 25

country-by-country approach, to COD Aid, 28

criticism, of foreign aid, 4, 6

D

data quality audit, required by GAVI, 98

decisionmakers, process approach requiring access to, 82

deforestation, in developing countries, 101

delays, in applying tests and submitting reports, 71

deliverables, paying fixed prices for, 11

democracy, promoting, 102

demographic variation, under a COD agreement, 94

developing countries

    COD Aid payments to, 56–57

    COD Aid working in most low income, 25–26

    deforestation in, 101

    ownership by, 12

development, foreign aid undermining, 4–5

Development Assistance Committee Network on Development Evaluation, 41

disaggregation level, in a COD Aid contract, 59

disclosure, levels of required in a COD Aid contract, 59

dissemination, public, 49

divergent objectives, of funders and recipients, 9

diversion of resources, caused by COD Aid, 32

domestic researchers, insights and experiences of, 85

DTP-3 (diphtheria, tetanus, and pertussis), 36, 98

E

economic recession, effect on foreign aid, 3

education. *See also* primary education; upper secondary education, COD Aid in international aid
    to, 31

education data, incentives to improve, 59

education goal, for a COD Aid agreement, 114

education sector

    applying COD Aid for goals beyond primary completion, 97

    COD (Cash on Delivery) Aid agreement, 46, 47

education system, facilitating public debate about, 49

Emergency Fund for AIDS Relief (PEPFAR), 98–99

empirical equating, 50

ENLACE *(Evaluación Nacional del Logro Académico en Centros Escolares)*, 93 environment, improving and preserving, 100–101

escrow, placing funds in, 68

European Commission, performance-linked budget support, 38

European Union, budget support to other governments, 6

Evaluación Nacional del Logro Académico en Centros Escolares (ENLACE), 93

exchange rates, inflated by aid inflows, 4

exit, problem of, 14

experimentation, COD Aid fostering, 25

expertise, using existing, 65

external shocks, 35

external validity, confirming in research, 81

F

Fast Track Initiative for Education, 72

federal government (Mexico)

    auditing state government accounts, 95

    improvements in upper secondary schools, 89–90

    programs addressing challenges, 90–91

Financial Accountability reports, of the World Bank, 33

financial arrangements, for a COD Aid agreement, 67–68

financial rewards, staking on test performance, 52

financing, adverse events and, 71

fiscal transfers, from central governments, 87

fixed-price contract, 10, 11, 12

foreign aid

    as a big and difficult business, 3

    challenges to, 3

    commitments, abiding by all existing, 69

    compared to intranational fiscal transfers, 88

    cost-reimbursement approach used for, 10–11

    criticism of, 4, 6

    as difficult to do well, 8–10

    efforts to reform, 6–8

    failure to disburse, 35

    growth of, 3, 4

    modalities, influence on institutions and governance, 80

    modifying for legitimate or illegitimate goals, 9

    necessity to generate measurable progress, 3

    new approach, 38–40

    predictability of, 8

principal-agent problem in, 10–14

programs, COD Aid displacing, 30

scaling up, 29–30

steering away from specific projects, 6

system

    articulating and reforming, 8

    failings of current, 5

    shortcomings of current, 4

undermining local institutional development, 87

foreign researchers, perspectives and experiences of, 85

fragile states

COD Aid in, 25–26

limitation of aid to, 14

with new and effective leaders, 26

reasons for success of COD Aid, 26

funder-recipient relationships, altering in COD Aid, 17

funders. *See also* private funders; public funders

accountability, 21

aid programs weakly accountable to, 8–9

baseline information, collection and analysis, 78

coordination, 27–28, 29

cost overruns, risking, 11

costs, covering direct, 20

countries, rewarding well performing, 68

discipline, 27

hands-off approach in COD Aid, 19

implementing agencies, compared to, 67

number of, increase in, 9

number of fragmenting public support for aid, 3

objectives of, 79

outcomes, incentives to invest in good data on, 25

principal-agent model, behavior under, 79–80

recipients

    agreement with, 112–114

    compensating for cost of testing, 54

    not precluded from engaging, 74

    undermining decision making of, 23

reducing administrative burden on, reducing, 29

roles changed by COD Aid, 23

test development, providing financial resources for, 51

    tradeoffs of, 39

    types of, 67

    verification agent, contract with, 116

funding

    COD Aid agreements, 67–71

    pooled from many sources, 73

G

Germany, projects in Tanzania (2007), 29

Global Alliance for Vaccines and Immunisation (GAVI), 36, 98

global compact, COD Aid as, 28

Global Partnership on Output-Based Aid, of the World Bank, 100

global price, 54

goal

    as an essential element of a COD Aid contract, 45–46

    of universal primary completion, 46–48

government, as accountable to foreign funders, 4

government performance, clear measures of, 7

government programs, scope for good quantitative analyses, 77

grant funding, to eradicate polio, 70

grantor, in a COD Aid agreement, 69

grants

    in COD Aid, 69–71

    conditions for, 6

H

health sector, applying COD Aid to, 98–100

HIV/AIDS

    approach to treating and preventing, 99

    prevention policies, funds diverted from in Mexico, 58

I

immunization coverage, baseline in Kenya, 98

immunization programs, expanding and improving, 36

Immunization Services Support program, 98

implementation

    of COD Aid agreements, 71–74

    tracing, 84

implementers, process approach requiring access to, 82

implementing agencies, distinguished from funders, 67

incentive(s)

  choosing a simple, 64

  payment of $200 per student as sufficient, 54

  power of, 19

  providing sums substantial enough, 54–55

incentive structure, influence of, 75

incidence rate, directly measuring, 99

incremental measures of progress, paying against, 38

incremental payment, 36

independent audit, in COD Aid, 20

independent third party, COD Aid verified by, 38

independent verification, for COD Aid progress, 19

indicators

  linking payments to overall performance, 37

  outcome, 99–100

  simple versus sophisticated, 64

information, asymmetry of between federal and state, 87

information systems

  as core requirement of good governance, 26

  reimbursing for creating, 32

infrastructure, expanding and improving, 100

innovation

  documenting and evaluating, 75

  inducing, 34

Innovation Fund. *See also* Upper Secondary Education Innovation Fund, proposed for Fast Track
  Initiative, 73

innovative approaches, fragile states responding to, 26

inputs, federal and state programs focusing on, 90

institution-building, COD Aid encouraging, 23

interests, divergence between federal and state, 87

International Development Association (IDA), 70

International Development Department and Associates (2006) report, 41

international programs, private giving for, 3

interviews

  with important actors in the process, 83

  prior to implementation of COD Aid agreement, 82

intranational fiscal transfers

  compared to foreign, 87

  feasible approach for, 95

  officials on both sides accountable, 88

investments, providing funds for initial, 31

Ireland, projects in Tanzania (2007), 29

J

Joint Evaluation of General Budget Support, 41

L

Laboratorio Latinoamericano student assessments, language arts test, 89

learning, standardized test of, 50

learning by doing, 25

lender, in a COD Aid agreement, 69

loans

    buying down, 70

    in COD Aid, 69–71

    conditions for, 6

local capacity, building, 23

local ownership, of policies and programs, 22

local production function, effect of asymmetric information on, 9

M

macro level, COD Aid attracting, 37

management, aid programs competing for people skilled in, 4

management information and testing systems, encouraging, 50–51

MDG Contracts, European Community's, 102

measurement instruments, 50

measures, of government performance, 7

methodologies, studying implementation of a policy, 84

Mexicanos Primero, 94, 95

Mexico

    advantages facilitating COD approach, 94

    funds diverted from HIV/AIDS prevention policies, 58

    upper secondary education in, 89–95

Millennium Challenge Account funds, 68

Millennium Challenge Corporation, 72

Millennium Development Goals

    commitment to, 3, 14

    universal primary education as one, 46

multilateral agency, 72

multilateral initiative, in the education sector, 72

N

narrative, testing against alternative explanations, 81–82

national identification number, 60

national learning assessments, 50–51

nongovernmental organizations (NGOs), 21

nonprofit initiatives, freedom to engage with, 24

Norway, projects in Tanzania (2007), 29

Norwegian government, first contributor to Amazon Fund, 101

O

objectives
   of budget support programs, 37
   divergence between funders and recipients, 9
   of funders, 79

official aid, 3, 14. *See also* foreign aid

official aid system, changing, 35

open contract, 71

outcome indicators, 99–100

outcome measure, verifying, 73

outcomes
   focusing on, 5
   funder's ability to report on, 27
   linking foreign assistance to, 21
   measuring for COD Aid, 20, 34, 35
   reporting, 21, 35, 52
   specifying, 11

output-based aid, 36–37

outputs, paying for, 37

P

Paris Declaration (2005), 8, 27, 39

payments
   attaching to average scores, 91
   basing on number of children taking exam, 52
   in COD Aid, 20
   conditions for, 115
   determining size of, 53–55, 56, 57
   to a developing country, 56–57
   elaborating on the structure of, 64
   formula for calculating, 55

for implementing testing, 54, 55

related to overall performance, 37

relaxing constraints, 53

timing of, 115

performance

clear measures of government, 7

focusing on results and outcomes, 8

of students in upper secondary school, 90, 93–94

performance audit, required for COD Aid, 19

philanthropic foundations, concerned with education in Mexico, 94

pilot experiences, differing from subsequent efforts, 84

policy conditionality loans, 11

policy dialogue, as demand-driven, 74

policy-based loans, 7, 11

policymaking, evidence base for effective, 50

polio transmission worldwide, campaign to eliminate, 70

political risks, of COD Aid, 35

pooled fund, for COD Aid, 28

Poverty Reduction Strategy Paper, 6, 38

prevalence rate, for HIV/AIDS, 99

primary education, applying COD Aid to, 45–74

primary school, completing, 48

principal-agent model, 79

principal-agent problem

between federal and state governments, 87

in foreign aid, 10–14

private and nonprofit initiatives, freedom to engage with, 24

private funders, COD Aid attracting, 27

prize money, treating COD Aid funds as, 68

prize system, proportional-reward, 34

prizes, structuring payment as, 35

process approach, 81–85

process conditions, as an approach to foreign aid, 6

process tracing, 83

program inputs, focusing on, 5

Programme for International Student Assessment, 61, 66

progress. *See also* unit of progress

measures of, 11

measuring and verifying, 46

overestimating, 98

public reports of, 55, 58

unit of, 20

verifying for COD Aid, 19

ways of verifying, 65

proportional-reward prize system, 34

public audit reports, 62

public contract, accepting, 39

Public Expenditure Reports, of the World Bank, 33

Public Expenditure Reviews, of the World Bank, 33

public financial accountability, standards for, 33

public funders, budget cycles precluding long term commitments, 67–68

public scrutiny, encouraging, 19

public services, disseminating information about, 58

public-private partnership, for progress, 73

Q

quality improvement, in education, 97

R

raw data, disclosure to researchers, 59

recipients

accountable primarily to funders under budget support, 38

administrative burden on, 9

aid programs and policies weakly accountable to, 9

bearing less risk under cost-reimbursement contracts, 11

behavior under principal-agent model, 80

COD Aid agreement with funders, 112–114

COD Aid giving more discretion to, 24

COD Aid making more accountable to citizens, 21

collection and analysis of baseline information on, 78

as composite of many actors, 80

directing funding to better-off areas or groups, 32

with discretion and responsibility in COD Aid, 19

factors beyond control of, 35

failure to make progress as problematic for, 35

focus on response of, 78

funders weakly accountable to, 9

incentives to invest in good data on outcomes, 25

maximizing effectiveness of programs, 29

measuring outcomes, 20

negotiating COD Aid for, 28

ownership by, 12

paying for successful public programs, 33

reducing administrative burden on, 27, 28, 29

responsibility and discretion for COD Aid, 22–25

responsibility fostering local involvement and accountability, 24

resulting actions affecting actual outcomes, 76

rewarding for progress when success is due to other causes, 33

roles changed by COD Aid, 23

taking action to progress, 20

tradeoffs of, 39

using local knowledge to assess technical assistance, 24

reforms, in the Paris Declaration, 8

reporting

for COD Aid agreement, 55, 58–62

effectiveness and credibility of, 94

reports, delays in submitting, 71

research

framework, 76

implementing COD Aid, 20

levels of, 76–79

methodology, 81

methods, 81

opportunities, 76

process approach, 81–85

purpose of, 76–79

strategies, 78, 79

unit of analysis for, 81

research team, qualifications for, 85–86

researchers

including both foreign and domestic, 85

as very familiar with the country, 82

responsibility, benefits generated by recipient, 23

results-based aid programs, building on, 36–38

results-based approaches, for health sector grants, 102

retest, of random sample of schools, 60

revenue collection, aid reducing incentives, 4

reward shares, 98

risk, viewing lack of disbursements as, 35

risks, for political leaders, 55

Rotary International/United Nations Foundation, buying down IDA loans, 70

S

samples, tests based on representative, 50

school enrollment, expanding at expense of quality, 32

schooling, quality, 49

schools, retesting a random sample of, 60–61

self-discovery, aid interrupting, 5

shared information, lack of, 10

simplicity, principles of, 64

social audits, 55, 58

sophisticated indicators, 64

South Africa, 58, 59

Southern African Consortium for Monitoring Educational Quality, 66

stakeholders, effects of new policies and programs on, 84

standardized testing, introducing, 97

standards-based assessments, 50

state governments, in Mexico, 89

states (Mexico)

    as subnational entities, 95

    use of funds by, 94

statistical comparisons, in research, 81

statistics, improving quality of, 101–102

student completions and test scores, payments for, 92–93

students

    purposes of testing, 51

    unique identifying number for each, 60

surveys, revealing understanding of new education strategy, 84

Sweden, projects in Tanzania (2007), 29

T

Tanzania, number of projects by donor (2007), 29

targets, specifying, 11

technical assistance, as demand-driven, 24, 74

technical support, contracting for, 51

term sheets

    development of, 111

    model, 112–117

test(s)

    care in using, 51–52

    design and administration, 59

    development and implementation, 52

    permitting delays in applying, 71

    teaching to, 51

test scores

    conditioning payments on, 52

    validity of, 51–52

testing

    initial payments for implementing, 54, 55

    measuring what society wants children to learn, 51

    payments to implement, 55

tied aid, 5, 79

tradeoffs, of moving to COD Aid, 39

transaction costs, of foreign aid system, 5

transparency

    achieved by COD Aid, 19

    COD Aid requiring, 21

    increased by an open contract, 71

    increasing, 102

    promoted by a global compact, 28

2005 Paris Declaration, 8, 27, 39

U

Uganda, community-based monitoring of health care, 58

U.K. Department for International Development, 68

U.K. government, providing budget support to other governments, 6

UN Millennium Declaration, universalizing primary school, 46

uniform payment, in a global compact, 28

unique identification, required for an accurate audit, 60

unit of analysis, for research, 81

unit of progress, 20, 46, 48–53, 93

United States, projects in Tanzania (2007), 29

universal primary completion, 46–48

upfront funding, COD Aid exclusion of, 32

upper secondary education, in Mexico, 89–90

Upper Secondary Education Innovation Fund, 90, 91

upper secondary schools (Mexico)

    COD Aid working, 91–95

    graduation rate from, 89

    poor performance in, 90

student completion and performance in, 93–94

U.S. Millennium Challenge Account, 22, 41

V

validity of test scores, 51–52

variable tranche, of EC budget support, 38

verification, for COD Aid agreement, 55, 58–62

verification agent

    compensation of, 116

    contract with funders, 116

    described, 111

    duties of, 112–113, 114, 115, 117

verification report, specification of, 117

Vietnam, administrative costs of aid to recipients, 5

vital statistics, COD Aid agreement aimed at improving, 102

volatility, in foreign aid, 5

W

waste, COD and, 33–34

windfall payments, under COD Aid, 33

working group, funder and recipient establishing, 76–77

World Bank

    allocating concessional funding, 6

    Global Partnership on Output-Based Aid, 100

    implementing polio eradication programs, 70

    technical advisory services from, 40

 Center
for Global
Development